HOUSEHOLD
secrets

Frances Halahan

NATIONAL TRUST BOOKS

This book is inspired by the National Trust's highly acclaimed illustrated survey *Looking After Antiques*, and as such benefits from the knowledge and expertise of the large number of conservators and specialists who contributed to that book. I would particularly like to thank Sarah Staniforth for her detailed reading and commenting on the text. *Frances Halahan*

First published in Great Britain in 2006 by National Trust Books

Illustrations by James Robins and Matt Windsor
Printed and bound by Kyodo Printing Co PTE, Singapore

Contents

4 Introduction

16 Ceramics

32 Metals

58 Textiles & Carpets

80 Furniture

98 Paper, Prints & Drawings

115 Floors

126 Index

Introduction

This book aims to help you look after your possessions so that you can keep them looking good and help prevent them from deteriorating. The more you know about objects, what they are made from and what happens to them through the course of their life, the easier it is for you to recognise problems and assess conditions.

Once signs of deterioration and possible treatments are identified, you will be well placed to decide whether changing the conditions in which the object is kept will sort out the problem, or whether you need to call on conservation advice. For example, if you want to clean a piece of sculpture without harming it, you will need to know what it is made from, its condition, the type of dirt that is removed, and whether or not a cleaning process is likely to cause damage. Understanding materials and what damage can be caused by different treatments is complex and if you are in any doubt, or your object is valuable or very important to you, do nothing and seek conservation advice.

Conservation & Restoration

In English-speaking countries, conservation and restoration refer to two distinct processes, although both are concerned with the care of objects. The purpose of conservation is to slow down the rate at which materials and objects deteriorate by taking preventive measures to limit the factors that cause decay and so reduce the risk of damage.

How this book works

In this book I deal with some of the most common materials found in the home, in the following six categories:

Ceramics
Metals
Textiles and carpets
Furniture
Paper, prints and drawings
Floors

For each one I take you through the Problems commonly associated with the material, followed by the methods of preventive conservation, ie, **Handling**, **Display and Storage**, **Housekeeping and Maintenance**, before outlining remedial conservation in **Cleaning** and **Repair**.

Health & Safety

For your own safety and peace of mind, make sure you obtain and read the health and safety advice from all the products you use. All chemicals, equipment and machinery should be treated with respect.

Problems

There are a number of factors that work towards the disintegration of materials and these can be divided into two groups. The first includes fire, flood and theft and is potentially disastrous while the second is more insidious, causing cumulative damage that can become critical if not controlled.

PHYSICAL DAMAGE

Scratches, chips, cracks, tears and dents can occur on objects from handling, moving, day-to-day use, inadequate support or packing while in store or on display, vigorous cleaning, inappropriate repair or accidents during building work. Protection against physical damage is generally a matter of common sense and thinking ahead to anticipate problems.

PESTS

Birds and rodents can severely damage or destroy objects by eating or shredding them to make a nest, or by staining them with urine and faeces. The nests of rodents and birds also harbour insects that can move into your collection. Materials most at risk are organic ones. Insects can be a major problem, but the most effective protection against insect infestation is regular housekeeping and making sure that textiles are clean before being put away. There is some evidence that high doses of lavender and cedarwood oil act as insect repellents, and there are now similar insect repellents commercially available in sachets.

LIGHT

Visible and ultraviolet light not only change the colour of some materials but can be very destructive too. Organic materials, particularly textiles and paper, are badly damaged by light: it causes colour change and eventually makes the material itself break up. This can often be seen on the backs of curtains, or the top of upholstered chairs by a window, where the fabric has disintegrated into ribbons. The surface of lacquer and japanning can become dull as it disintegrates and furniture can be made paler or darker by light, depending on the wood. Light damage is cumulative and can be caused by artificial light as well as daylight. Direct sunlight is the most damaging. There are a number of things that can be done to reduce light damage:

- Hang roller blinds and/or curtains to cut out direct sunlight and reduce general levels of daylight.
- Use loose covers on upholstered furniture.
- Place light-sensitive objects in darker parts of a room. Corridors and halls often have dimmer lighting, so can be more suitable for, say, photographs and watercolours, than living rooms.
- Paint a room in pale colours – this means it will need less artificial lighting.
- Use ultraviolet absorbing filters to cut down light damage. The filters can be placed over windows and light sources or on picture glass and make no obvious difference to the appearance of the room, as they are clear.

HUMIDITY

The air around us contains water vapour. High humidity causes metals to corrode, mould to form, wood and other organic materials to swell, veneers to lift and also provides an environment attractive to insects. Low humidity makes organic materials shrink and split or cockle. Textiles and paper may become brittle and furniture joints loosen. Again, veneers may lift (in this case because glue desiccates and ceases to be effective).

Fluctuating humidity – produced when central heating goes on and off, for example – causes organic materials to change dimension. This is problematic with objects of more than one material, as the materials will swell and contract at different rates. Wood may do so more than the paint on its surface, eventually causing a separation along the join of the wood and the paint so that the paint begins to flake.

Humidity is measured as relative humidity and is altered by temperature changes in a room. When cold air is heated, the relative humidity will drop and become lower than the air outside. When central heating goes on and off during the course of the day, this causes the relative humidity to fall and rise. The relative humidity near a radiator is usually low and not the place for furniture and paintings.

TEMPERATURE

Most materials are unaffected by the normal range of room temperatures but a few materials cannot withstand certain temperatures. The most obvious example is wax, which melts at quite low temperatures. A brief spell in sunshine can destroy a wax figure or fruit. Freezing temperatures can damage stone, terracotta and other porous materials if they are wet before becoming frozen.

POLLUTION AND CHEMICAL DAMAGE

Gases, dust and dirt are all forms of pollution that can disfigure or damage materials. The gases come from pollution in the atmosphere and from certain materials like wood, paint and cardboard. Little can be done to protect objects from pollution produced externally, but you can protect them against being damaged by inappropriate storage or display materials. For this reason you will see recommendations throughout the book to use acid-free or archival quality materials. These cause less damage than non-archival storage or display products such as mounting board, cardboard, newsprint or PVC, which may give off damaging acids.

Particulate pollution or dust comes mainly from carpets, concrete floors, unsealed walls and other construction work, pets and even people who shed skin, hair and fibres. Dust and dirt on objects looks unpleasant, but the more an object is cleaned the more the surface may be worn away. Dust can also encourage corrosion of metals and damage to other materials. If you protect your objects from dust by covering and packing them when they are not being used, you will avoid having to constantly clean them. Well-fitting windows and doors will keep out pollution and dust, and display cases and glazed framing will protect on the inside, although it is nicer to have some of your collection open.

BIODETERIORATION

Mould or fungi, algae or lichen can grow on objects. Algae, lichen and moss are found on stone, wood, metal and other materials displayed outside. Mould will grow on any damp organic material and on some inorganic materials if there is enough dust and dirt for them to thrive. The main problem with mould is staining – brown, orange, blue, white or black spots form on the surface, and sometimes long hairs.

If mould appears on an object, the first thing to do is to change the conditions in which the piece is kept. Either move the object to a drier room, or improve matters within the room, particularly the air circulation.

INHERENT DETERIORATION

The manufacturing process used to make some objects, or the materials used in objects, can leave them inherently unstable and prone to deterioration. For example, cellulose nitrate, a widely used early plastic often produced to imitate ivory and tortoiseshell as well as being used for early film stock, gradually deteriorates, giving off corrosive nitric acid. Some glass can be unstable and may 'weep' and gradually disintegrate while cheap paper made from wood pulp produces acids that destroy the paper. This deterioration is impossible to stop and the best remedy is to keep these objects in the best possible conditions.

Handling

Handling objects safely is mostly a matter of common sense and thinking ahead. The rule of thumb is to handle objects as infrequently as possible. Also make sure you remove rings, watches, long necklaces and other items that may scratch or catch on the object.

If you do have to move an object, prepare an appropriate space to receive it. Ensure that your route is clear, free of electrical flexes or other obstacles, and have another person open the doors for you. Before picking the object up, check carefully for weaknesses such as cracks, old repairs, vulnerable parts, and remove anything detachable, such as lids.

Make sure that your hands are clean before you touch an object and always wear gloves when handling metals, gilded frames and furniture. Gloves will protect the objects from the skin's salts and oils – these deposits can cause materials to mark or corrode. Fingerprints will gather dirt and leave unsightly marks.

Display & Storage

Finding a safe place to display your objects largely comes down to common sense. Choose a spot where they cannot easily be knocked against or onto the floor and which is not too dry or damp.

Objects that stand on the floor, whether in store or on display, should be placed on battens or a plinth so that they are raised a few centimetres above the floor. This means you can clean the floor without harming the object, and makes it easier to move the item.

Where possible, use acid-free or archival quality materials to make the support for displaying objects and for storage materials. Cover objects in store with acid-free or archival tissue paper, a clean dustsheet, washed calico or Tyvek. Alternatively pack them in archival-quality boxes with acid-free tissue padding and protect them from dust, pollution and physical damage.

Only leave objects packed in Bubblewrap or polyethylene foam for more than a few days if they are in a good environment that is not damp, otherwise mould or corrosion can occur from lack of air circulation.

- **Dust and dirt** – are the objects being cleaned too much? Is the dirt loosely attached or firmly stuck on? Are there already signs of damage from over-cleaning?
- **Insects** – these like dark and undisturbed places, such as pockets and folds of clothes and backs of furniture. Are there signs of infestation, such as frass, larvae skins, clothes-moth webbing, holes, chewed areas or even insects, dead or alive?
- **Deterioration** – look for colours fading or changing, mould or damp stains, flaking or lifting paint, cracks in the wood, lifting veneers, corrosion or tarnish of metals, unravelling fringes on upholstery, finger marks, scratches and dents.
- **Decoration** – look for any form of decoration that could be damaged by treatment, such as paint, applied gems and niello, or decoration that might be pulled off by cleaning, such as inlay or gold leaf.

Cleaning

There are two levels of cleaning objects. The first is routine general housekeeping, to maintain the appearance of an object. The second is carried out less regularly, and is more likely to improve significantly the appearance of the object. Typically, an object might undergo the second level of cleaning when newly acquired if it is grimy. After that, the first level of cleaning should be enough.

FIRST LEVEL OF CLEANING/GENERAL HOUSEKEEPING

Always check that the object is sound before starting to clean it. The best way to remove dust from objects is by 'dust vacuuming'. Once you get used to it, this is a quick and thorough technique.

- Hold a brush of ponyhair or hogshair and flick the dust off into the nozzle of a vacuum cleaner, which you hold with your other hand.
- Swap the brush for a clean one when it is dirty, and make sure that the metal ferrule does not scratch the surface by binding it with self-adhesive tape.

Don't be tempted to use the brush attachment of the vacuum cleaner directly on the object; the strong suction can be damaging and you cannot see what you are doing. If the object is unstable, you may need someone to hold it steady. Nylon net is usually placed over the nozzle for cleaning textiles, fragile painted surfaces and upholstered furniture. This prevents threads, paint flakes, tassels and other loose pieces from being sucked into the cleaner.

Dusters and microfibre cloths are used for polishing flat surfaces. A lint-free duster with hemmed edges is preferable to a fluffy duster with oversewn edges, as the fluff can get caught on objects and the oversewing can catch on raised areas and edges. Avoid feather dusters, as the feathers can break and scratch.

If pieces of an object such as flakes of paint or pieces of veneer come off during cleaning, keep them in a marked envelope until you can re-fix them or get help from a conservator.

SECOND LEVEL OF CLEANING

This should only be done occasionally. Before cleaning an object, assess what it is made from and its condition. If you are in any doubt about what can be done, leave it alone until you can get advice from a conservator – there is always danger of causing damage during cleaning. See each chapter for more details on cleaning.

Repair

Repairing objects, particularly furniture, can be complicated and difficult. For this reason, only simple repairs have been discussed in this book. It is advisable to get conservation help if you need to repair valuable, fragile or very special objects.

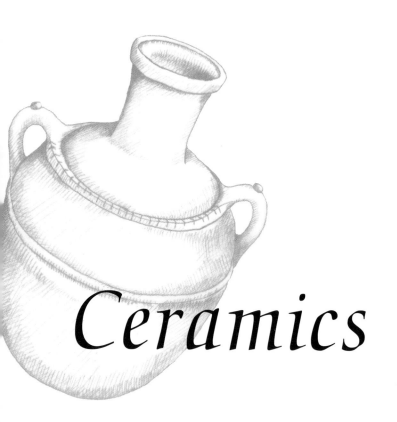

Ceramics

Ceramics is a term used to describe objects made from fired clay. It includes a wide range of objects, from flower pots, dinner services and figurines to external sculpture, drainpipes and electrical insulators, as well as many other items often referred to as pottery or china. The clay mixture and the temperature at which it is fired vary, and the resulting ceramic materials can range from being very soft and porous to hard and glasslike. Ceramics can be divided into three main groups:

- porcelain
- stoneware
- earthenware

Ceramics often have a glaze applied to the surface for decoration and strength. This is a thin glassy layer which, in the case of porous ceramics (earthenware), makes them non-porous so they can be used for holding liquids.

Earthenware is porous (it will absorb water or other liquids), can be quite soft and is often glazed. Unglazed earthenware, such as many archaeological and ethnographic wares, can be quite rough and coarse and are commonly the colour of clays: brown, red or grey.

Earthenware was frequently produced to imitate porcelain; a range of finely potted, cream-coloured, glazed earthenware called creamware was developed by Josiah Wedgwood in the 17th century to look like porcelain and was imitated by other Staffordshire factories. Other examples are Delftware and majolica – tin-glazed earthenware where an opaque white glaze was applied over an earthenware body and often decorated in blue.

Stonewares include celadons from China and the Far East, European salt-glazed stoneware and jasperware, pioneered by Wedgwood. It is non-porous and quite strong – the salt-glazed stoneware was used to make domestic and industrial objects such as cooking vessels and drainpipes.

True **porcelain** is referred to as hard-paste porcelain, and is a glassy, whitish material, often with a blue or greyish tone, and is slightly translucent. It was first made in China in about AD900. It was not until the 18th century that the secret of its manufacture was first discovered at Meissen in Germany. A few English factories made hard-paste porcelain, most notably Plymouth, Bristol and New Hall.

Soft-paste porcelain was made to imitate hard-paste porcelain – because the particular clay needed for hard-paste porcelain was not readily available in Europe – and is usually white and almost non-porous. It is slightly softer in appearance than hard-paste. The best known English factories producing this type of porcelain in the 18th century included Bow, Chelsea, Worcester and Derby.

Bone china was developed in England in the 19th century and is also a type of porcelain. It is white, quite durable and cheaper to produce than soft-paste porcelain.

Biscuit porcelain and **Parian ware** (*see* p.27) can be either soft- or hard-paste porcelain. They are usually white with a texture similar to marble and often used to make statuettes, sculpture and jewellery.

GLAZES
The glaze on a ceramic can be clear or coloured. Frequently, additional decoration is painted over the glaze and fired at a low temperature. These colours are sometimes referred to as enamel colours. Many ceramics have a basic blue underglaze design with details added as on-glaze decoration, sometimes gilded.

Problems
Being able to identify the type of ceramic you have, particularly whether it is earthenware or glazed earthenware, will help you care for it properly. In addition, you need to be able to know what problems or deterioration to look out for and establish what condition it is in. Most ceramics are very durable, but they are brittle and the glaze can become fragile.

You should look for:

* cracks, chips or breaks, including repaired breaks;
* old repairs that have discoloured or weakened;

'Spalling' on terracotta pots occurs when the water that has been absorbed freezes and expands

- on-glaze decoration, particularly on Staffordshire figures, that is starting to come off – you may see rough patches on the glaze where a colour is missing;
- a powdery or flaking surface decoration on unglazed ceramics – this can come off very easily with handling;
- marking and staining on delicate unglazed wares – oils in the skin may be absorbed by the ceramic when handling;
- staining on glazed earthenware. This can happen when the glaze has cracked or crazed and is often seen in blue and white Staffordshire domestic ware in which the body close to the cracks becomes stained from use – for instance, in jugs and tureens;
- deterioration of the glaze on a ceramic piece whereby it becomes cloudy or iridescent, or even flakes off. This is mostly seen on archaeological wares and Islamic ceramics;
- a whitish crust on the surface of plant containers and buried ceramics. This is caused by hard water and is similar to the scaling in a kettle. It may be disfiguring but is not harmful.

Handling

Most ceramics are durable but can easily be broken if handled incorrectly or jolted.

- Make sure you do not place your thumb on a leaf, petal or other delicate piece that could be snapped off.
- Do not pick objects up by their handles, knobs or rims, as they may be weak or may have been broken previously. Carry the object using both hands and support large plates under the centre, not by the rim.
- If possible, remove lids and loose parts before turning an object over.
- Wrap objects in good-quality tissue paper – not cotton wool.
- Wear thin latex or nitrile gloves when handling unglazed wares or where the glaze is flaking off, as this can be pulled off on your fingers.

Display

When choosing where to display your ceramics, look for a place where they will be secure and not be knocked by closing doors, flapping curtains, cats or people. Choose somewhere that doesn't get too dusty so that the pieces do not have to be cleaned too regularly.

- Check the bases of objects before putting them on polished furniture – rough undersides can scratch the polish. If necessary, make pads from chamois leather, cork, felt or polyethylene foam to place under the object.

Soluble Salts

These are white, powdery or needle-like crystals that form on the surface of glazed or unglazed objects, or along the cracks in the glaze of some wares, and which weaken the body or the surface. They are often found on plant containers.

The salts occur when the ceramic absorbs certain chemicals dissolved in water. Then, when the object is dry and the humidity low, the salts crystallise out, forming white deposits. If the humidity changes, a cycle of crystallisation occurs, which causes the surface of the ceramic to break up and be come powdery, or pushes off the glaze. A common source of soluble salts is inappropriate cleaning with chlorine-containing bleaches. You should therefore avoid domestic bleach when cleaning ceramic objects.

- Plates and tiles in good condition can be hung on the wall using plastic-coated metal hangers, but make sure that the hanger is the correct size, otherwise it may damage the object.
- Where possible, use a metal or plastic liner inside any ceramic vessel you use as a flower vase or plant-holder.
- Glass-fronted cabinets are good places for ceramics, as they protect them from dust and physical damage.

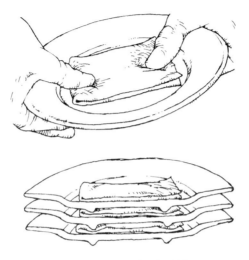

Stacking plates interleaved with acid-free paper

Storage

When storing ceramics, keep them in a clean, dry area and protect them from dust, either by wrapping in acid-free tissue and storing in a box or by covering with acid-free tissue paper 'hats' while on a shelf. If you are storing a lot of ceramics and glass objects, it is better to try to keep them on closely spaced, fairly narrow shelves rather than wide shelves so that you do not have to reach over several objects to retrieve something from the back. Try to keep the smaller objects at the front and avoid stacking cups and bowls, as they may stick together or may break.

ceramics

Housekeeping & Maintenance

Ceramic objects need to be cleaned from time to time and the most effective way is to dust the surface using a soft brush, provided the surface is not flaking or very fragile, in which case you should ask advice from a conservator.

Cleaning

Occasionally your ceramics will need more than just dusting. It's important in this case to distinguish between those objects that can be put in water, and those that can't. With earthenware, glazed earthenware and restored pieces, for example, problems can occur. To be on the safe side, do not wash any object you think is rare, very old, fragile or precious; they should be cleaned by a conservator or following conservation advice.

To assess your ceramic for cleaning purposes, first examine it carefully to make sure it is in good condition, and that it has not been previously restored. Then determine whether it is earthenware, glazed earthenware, porcelain or stoneware. Remove all dust with a brush – a hogshair brush should be suitable.

! Never wash old ceramics or ceramics decorated with gilding in a dishwasher, as the heat and chemicals used in the washing process can bleach some glaze colours, may remove the gold and can damage the glaze.

The method used for the next stage of cleaning will depend on the type of ceramic and its condition.

WASHING PORCELAIN AND STONEWARE
Provided they are in good condition, porcelain and stoneware objects can be immersed in water. You should wash the objects one at a time in a plastic bowl large enough to take the entire object.

1 Fill the bowl with warm water and add a few drops of a conservation-grade detergent.
2 Use a hogshair brush to remove dirt.
3 Lift the object from the bowl, put it down nearby, throw away the water.
4 Refill the bowl and rinse the object well in clean warm water.
5 Remove the object from the bowl and pat it dry with paper towels or a soft cloth.
6 Allow to dry in a warm place.

WASHING CERAMICS THAT CANNOT BE PUT IN WATER
Glazed earthenware such as creamware, tin-glazed earthenware, objects with deteriorated glaze or overglaze, gilded objects, objects with metal mounts or objects which have been repaired can often be cleaned using water and cotton wool buds.

These objects can be 'washed' but not immersed in water. Water is not allowed to run under the glaze, preventing staining or other damage.

1 Place the object on a table that has been covered with a towel or similar padding and brush off the dust with a soft brush. An artist's hogshair paintbrush may be useful for cleaning ornate decoration. If the surface is rough, use a hogshair brush rather than cotton swab.

2 Support the object with one hand and use a cotton bud dampened with water containing a few drops of conservation-grade detergent. 'Rinse' with a bud or brush dipped in clean water.

3 Pat with paper towels or soft cloth to remove surface water and allow to dry in a warm place.

Objects with metal mounts can be cleaned as described above, but the metal should not get wet and the object should be dried straight away.

CLEANING CERAMICS THAT SHOULD NEVER GET WET

Unglazed earthenware, terracotta, painted ceramics or very deteriorated ceramics with flaking glaze or iridescence should be cleaned using dry methods only. Use a hogshair brush or soft artist's brush to remove the dust and dirt, but take care not to remove the glaze or paint. If you think the glaze is coming off, stop cleaning and get advice from a conservator. Equally, if you want the object to be cleaned more thoroughly, take it to a ceramics conservator.

CLEANING BISCUIT AND PARIAN WARE

The matt surface of biscuit porcelain and Parian ware makes them difficult to clean, but provided the objects are in good condition they can be washed as described for porcelain. It may help to remove the dirt by brushing the surface with a stencil brush. If washing does not clean the object, you may be able to remove the dirt using a white spirit/water mixture or other water/solvent mixtures and rinsing with clean water. If this is unsuccessful, consult a ceramics conservator.

Repair

Ceramics can be repaired with an easily reversible adhesive. If you break an object that you would like to have professionally repaired or that you want to keep until you have more time, collect all the pieces and wrap them individually in acid-free tissue and store in a box. This keeps them clean and protects them from further damage. Unglazed earthenware is very soft and must be treated with great care during preparation and repair.

Successful repairs do demand a lot of time and patience, so it is advisable to have objects that are precious to you repaired by a professional ceramics conservator.

A repair will look good only if the surfaces of the break are well prepared and you have checked that the pieces join tightly, otherwise there will be an unpleasant gap along the break. Before sticking anything together, therefore, all the surfaces to be joined must be clean and the old adhesive removed. If the object is recently broken, this is not a problem, although it is important not to handle the break edges and make them dirty: the dirt will not show until the pieces are joined together.

If there are a number of pieces to be joined, you will need to work out the order in which the pieces go together so that, in the process of reassembling, one section will not be locked out. You can either assemble the object by sticking all the pieces onto the largest piece and building the object up slowly, or by sticking several pairs of pieces together and then fitting the pairs to each other. In both cases the final pieces may no longer go well together if the other joins are not quite perfect, and you will have to start again.

1 Apply a small amount of the easily reversible adhesive along one break edge and push the pieces together tightly. Use enough adhesive to cover the surface of one of the joins but not too much, or the excess will dribble down the object.

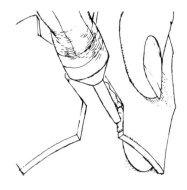

2 Make sure the pieces are well aligned by running your fingernail over the break. It should feel smooth.

3 Hold the pieces in place until the adhesive has set. Provided the surface is sound, you can use self-adhesive tape on both sides for this.

4 Use a bowl of uncooked rice or lentils for propping up pieces while they set. Bowls of sand are an alternative, but the sand always seems to get stuck in the joins.

5 Leave for 12 hours or more before adding on the next piece.

If there is a little excess adhesive pushing out of the sides of the join, let it dry and then cut it off carefully with a scalpel. If there is a lot of excess, remove it with a clean tissue before it sets. Try not to 'wash' it off with solvent, as this may weaken the join

or may wash the adhesive into the body of the object, thereby discolouring it. Once the adhesive is dry, you can remove any smeary areas by wiping with a cotton swab barely dampened with acetone.

If your repair is not satisfactory, soften the adhesive with acetone and clean the pieces before starting again.

Ceramic Tiles

Wall and floor tiles are often made from ceramics – sometimes high-fired stoneware but more often glazed earthenware. Individual ceramic tiles create an attractive display. Contemporary tiles are often manufactured with a perforation in the back to take picture wire or plastic-coated wire, which makes displaying them very easy, but older tiles are not so accommodating. You can buy hangers that stick on the back of the tile, but these are not recommended because the tile back is seldom smooth and so the pads do not stick well. And, of course, the adhesive may fail and the tile go crashing to the ground. Non-adhesive plate hangers with a spring to hold it in place are more suitable.

Just make sure the plate hanger is the right size for the tile and avoid using it on tiles that are cracked or have been repaired, as the strain from the spring can cause a crack to become a break.

Displaying thin tiles

Even small cup hooks can be too big for some thin tiles, in which case you will need to use stainless-steel pins covered in thin plastic tube. The pins need to be long enough to allow at least 1.5cm (⅝in) to go into the board, plus the thickness of the tile, and to allow for at least 1cm (½in) of turn. If the pins have heads, these must be cut off with pliers. To make the right-angle turn, hold the pin with a pair of pliers and use long-nosed pliers to bend the pin at about 1cm (½in) from the end. Drill a very small hole into the mdf, using a needle-fine drill bit. Push the pin into the hole and make sure it is held tightly, then slip the plastic tube over the pin. Turn the pins outwards and place the tile in position, then turn the pins inwards to hold the tile in place. Use strong fixings and brass picture wire at the back of the panel or mirror plates when attaching the mounted tile to the wall.

Metals

M etals have been used throughout history to make a wide range of objects, including jewellery, cooking equipment, candlesticks, teapots, machinery, sculpture and toys. In this chapter I am covering the metals most commonly used historically and found in the home today – copper and its alloys, iron and steel, lead and pewter, silver, and tin.

Few metals are used in their pure form – they are mixed with other metals to make an alloy. An alloy improves a metal's appearance, working properties and strength, and is economic.

Steel	is an alloy of iron and carbon.
Pewter	is alloyed with tin, copper and lead.
Sterling Silver	is an alloy of silver and copper.
Copper	is alloyed with other metals, such as lead, tin and zinc, to make harder **bronze** and **brass**.

CORROSION (RUST)

When it comes to caring for and preserving metal objects in your home, the first thing to bear in mind is that all metals corrode (with the exception of pure gold). Oxygen and water vapour are needed for corrosion to develop and, depending on the metal, other agents such as sulphide gases and certain acids need to be present. Sulphur containing compounds such as hydrogen sulphide causes tarnishing and can be given off by people, wool and silk, organic matter and eggs. Rust is the same thing as corrosion, but the term 'rust' is used only for ferrous metals. Tarnish is a form of corrosion where a thin, smooth, coloured surface is formed on some polished metals, particularly silver and copper and its alloys.

Handling
- Our hands leave oil and moisture on any surface. Where possible, wear thin rubber, latex, vinyl, neoprene or nitrile gloves. Avoid cotton gloves.
- Adhesive tape and labels can cause metals to corrode or tarnish and can take off the patina when they are removed from bronze, lead and other surfaces. Use tie-on labels.
- Many candlesticks are made of a thin skin of metal filled with natural resin and/or plaster of Paris and are therefore much weaker than they look. Handle them carefully, supporting the weight from underneath.

Display & Storage
Keep your metal objects in fairly dry conditions. Small metal objects that corrode easily can be kept dry by storing them with silica gel in sealed plastic boxes. They will need to be inspected at regular intervals and the silica gel may need conditioning. Protect large objects from dust by using a dustsheet.

Housekeeping & Maintenance
Metal objects need dusting occasionally with a soft brush and vacuum cleaner, or use a dry microfibre cloth for flat objects. Check them at least

once a year for signs of active corrosion or tarnish. Silver, brass and copper are often protected from tarnish with a clear lacquer. These objects should also be checked occasionally for scratched, damaged or failing lacquer. (See individual metals for further advice.)

Cleaning

How often and how much you clean a metal object will depend on the metal, where it is placed and how you want it to look. Rare, old and precious objects should be cleaned only by a metals conservator. Excessive cleaning can damage the highly prized patina on bronze, remove decorative textures and engraving, or remove the plated metal coating on silver, thereby exposing the base metal.

REMOVING CANDLE WAX AND OLD WAX POLISH

Candle wax is easier to remove when it is chilled, as this makes it more brittle. So if you have wax on an object, place it in the fridge for about half an hour and then scrape off the wax with your fingernail, soft wood spatula or a bamboo stick. Do not use a metal scraper, as it will scratch. Remnants of wax can be removed with white spirit on a cotton wool swab. To chill the wax on larger objects, put some ice cubes in a bag and hold them against the wax.

Repair

The key to repairing metal is to use the appropriate methods and materials.

Minimising tarnish

Special tarnish-reducing cloth bags and pouches are available to keep silver shiny while not in use. You can also buy plastic bags to keep silver and other polished metals free of tarnish – these protect most metals against corrosion and change colour to indicate when the corrosion protection is no longer effective. Polished metal, such as silver, silver gilt and polished copper, tarnishes more rapidly if displayed over a radiator or fireplace. Wrapping polished metal objects in acid-free tissue paper will help fight tarnish, but do not wrap objects in cling film as some metals react with it over a period of time and will bond with it.

Ideally, repairs to metal objects should be carried out by an experienced metal conservator. If you do need to make a small repair, such as re-attaching a handle or putting a knob on a lid, use an epoxy resin or easily reversible adhesive, as most other methods (such as welding or using soft- or hard-solder) involve the use of heat, which can change or damage the object.

COPPER, BRONZE & BRASS

Copper is a soft, pinkish metal and is often alloyed with other metals to make it stronger. Brass and bronze are both alloys of copper.

Bronze is an alloy of copper and tin, frequently with lead and/or zinc. It is usually more pink and pale than brass. Bronzes often have a surface patina. This has either been applied deliberately or is a build-up of corrosion that has been allowed to develop. The colour of the patina can range from golden-brown through brownish-black to green. The patina is highly prized and should never be removed.

Brass is gold in colour and is an alloy of copper and zinc. It tends to be kept shiny and is often protected by a clear lacquer.

Pinchbeck is a type of brass with a lower percentage of zinc and looks very like gold.

Housekeeping & Maintenance
Remove dust with a soft brush or dry microfibre cloth. Brass fittings on antique furniture should not be polished to a high shine but wiped with a dry microfibre cloth and occasionally buffed with a metal polishing cloth. The shine on shiny metallic copper and brass can be maintained by rubbing occasionally with a soft cloth or metal polishing cloth.

Cleaning
Polish tarnished copper and brass with fine abrasive paste on a soft cloth, cotton wool swab or impregnated wadding. (Liquid copper and brass cleaners are not recommended, as they can cause problems if not removed

fully or if allowed to run behind or under an object.) Use a small piece of wadding cotton wool wrapped around a bamboo stick to clean small intricate areas. Wear vinyl, latex or nitrile gloves.

- Remove all the polish from cracks, joins and details because it can be disfiguring if allowed to build up.

- Remove old polish using a cotton bud moistened with alcohol or white spirit. Do not use a pin or sharp metal object. Remove the sludge with a soft cloth or cotton wool.

! Lemon juice or vinegar and salt are sometime suggested for cleaning copper and brass. These should be avoided, as they can damage the surface of the metal and leave brass looking very pink and coppery.

The area around a copper or brass plaque, or around door furniture, must be protected so that neither the polish nor cloth stray onto the surrounding material, as they will mark and stain in time.

Problems

- The polished metal tarnishes, becoming dull and eventually dark brown or even green.
- Copper and its alloys need polishing to keep them shiny, but this removes some of the metal! You can reduce the need to clean by keeping them away from areas where they will tarnish quickly, such as over a fireplace.
- In high humidity, if kept wet or when buried, copper and its alloys form red, blue or green corrosion.
- The metals are quite soft and may dent and scratch easily.
- Bronzes can be brittle and split or break if handled roughly.
- Some copper and copper alloy objects suffer from a rapid form of copper corrosion, which is sometimes referred to as 'bronze disease'. When this occurs, small dots of bright green corrosion form and these can grow quite rapidly if not treated.
- Polish that has been allowed to build up in crevices can cause corrosion of the metal and will gradually turn green.
- If the object is painted, lacquered or enamelled, seek conservation advice before cleaning.

Protection

Decorative brass and copper objects can be protected from tarnish by a lacquer. (Lacquer is not appropriate for domestic objects you handle regularly, as the lacquer will be scratched.) The lacquer should be applied professionally, as it is difficult to achieve a good finish.

Microcrystalline wax can be used in place of lacquer and this will give some level of protection. Apply the wax with a soft brush and polish with a lint-free cloth. Re-wax regularly; the frequency will depend on how much wear the object receives. Use white spirit on a cotton swab to remove the wax.

IRON & STEEL

Ferrous metals are distinguished from other metals because they are magnetic. Even quite corroded iron and steel objects can have an effect on a magnet. Both iron and steel have been used widely to make a variety of objects from arms and armour to industrial equipment, fire grates, railings and jewellery.

Iron is either cast or wrought, the main difference being that cast iron has a high carbon content, making it difficult to forge.

Cast iron is used to make ranges, fire backs, fire surrounds and some decorative objects. It is brittle and so breaks easily. It is also porous and can absorb quite a lot of water if it is left outside for a long time – drying can take several days.

Wrought iron is more malleable and hammered into patterns, twisted and curled when red hot to make items like gates, fire screens and wall lights.

Steel is an alloy of iron and carbon. Stainless steel also contains chromium and some other metals. Some stainless steels are not magnetic.

Problems

Rust (*see* p.33) is the scourge of ferrous metals, and iron and steel will rust very quickly in a damp atmosphere. Rust usually appears as spots or a light coating on the metal but can develop into thick flakes, and is a characteristic yellow, orange or brown. Various surface coatings have been applied to ferrous metals to help protect them against rust, including paint, wax, oil or graphite, which was used on kitchen ranges. Sometimes a layer of colour was deliberately applied – for example, gun barrels and clock hands were blued. The original coating may act as a corrosion deterrent and should not be cleaned or removed without conservation advice.

Housekeeping & Maintenance

Remove dust with a soft brush, dry microfibre cloth or soft, lint-free cloth.

General dirt and grime can usually be removed by wiping with cotton wool swabs moistened with alcohol or white spirit, although if the surface is painted it is best just to brush the dust off. Even a small amount of water can set off corrosion, so it is not generally used for cleaning. Once the surface is dry, protect with a light coating of wax (*see* Protection, p.43).

Cleaning

Heavily corroded iron, inlaid objects and objects with a decorated surface are difficult to clean well without damaging the metal or losing decoration. Steel grates and some other steel objects may have been gilded or have an engraved decoration that is not easily visible. Clean a small area first to check this and if in doubt ask for advice from a conservator.

REMOVING RUST

First check that the metal is not blued, browned or has a surface coating that will be damaged by cleaning.

Rust is usually removed mechanically, either with an abrasive or by cutting it off with a scalpel. This tends to be safer than using chemicals, which can change the surface colour or remove all the paint or bluing. When cleaning mechanically, it is easy to scratch the metal surface so the work must be carried out carefully and it may help to check that there is no damage by using magnification.

- Small spots of corrosion are best sliced or picked off with a scalpel or pin, particularly on painted or decorated surfaces where any treatments may damage the decoration. Use a slightly blunt scalpel with a rounded blade (eg 10 or 15) and keep it flat, almost parallel to the surface. A pin or needle can be held in a pin vice, which aids control when picking away at small spots.

- Where there is only a light coating of corrosion on a sound, metal surface, use a fine abrasive paste on a cotton wool swab, moving the swab in straight lines rather than in circles. Polish with a lint-free cloth.
- Remove more severe rust with fine wire wool (grade 000 or 0000) and fine abrasive paste. Again, rub the surface in straight lines, wipe off the slurry with white spirit, dry with a clean cloth or paper towels and repeat the process until the rust is removed.
- Where the corrosion is very thick, use a wire brush to take away the loose flakes and then clean with the fine wire wool and abrasive.

Original paint should not be removed, as it is an important part of the object's history. Stainless steel is easily scratched and should not be cleaned with wire wool or abrasives. Wash with warm soapy water, rinse and dry.

Protection
The cleaned ferrous metal must be protected as soon as possible after cleaning, otherwise it will start to rust again. Make sure you do not touch the metal with your bare hands before applying the protections. The protective coating can be paint, lacquer, wax or black lead.

- Steel should be left steel coloured unless it has been decorated by bluing, gilding or other surface finish. It and other ferrous metals that are to

43

retain their metal appearance can be waxed lightly with micro-crystalline wax applied with a brush and then polished with a soft, clean cloth.

- Make sure that the whole surface is coated, including the underneath and all crevices. Wax the object about once a year to maintain the protection.

- Use light machine oil with rust-inhibiting properties or gun oil to protect moving parts and hand tools. Apply a small quantity of oil on a clean cloth and take care not to get the oil on the wood or other organic materials, as it will stain. Remove the excess with a paper towel or clean, cotton cloth. The oil will need reapplying at regular intervals, but do not let a thick layer build up.

- If you are painting iron, chose a good-quality paint designed for use with iron and try to match the original gloss and colour. Prime the metal first with a primer that is compatible with the paint. Use the paint according to the manufacturers' instructions and make sure you leave enough time between coats for the paint to dry.

- Some objects, such as fire grates, get hot when used. Instead of paint, therefore, they are protected with black lead, a graphite paste traditionally used on stoves. Brush and then polish with a clean brush. Reapply as necessary.

LEAD, PEWTER AND BRITANNIA METAL

Lead is a grey, heavy metal that is shiny when freshly cut. Lead is toxic and can build up in the blood and damage your health. It will leave a black mark when rubbed on paper, and marks your hands, so make sure you always wash them after contact with lead.

Problems

* Lead is actually one of the least easily corroded of metals. However, if it is exposed to organic acid vapour produced by many woods and wood products – for example, from being stored in modern oak furniture, a creamy film of corrosion will develop and eventually the corrosion will distort the object.
* Lead sculptures often have a ferrous metal internal structure that can corrode. The corrosion can split the lead in some spots or cause the figure to be deformed.
* Pewter and lead are soft so easily dented or scratched.
* They can develop an attractive surface patina, but this is easily removed by careless handling and self-adhesive labels and tape.

Old pewter is an alloy of tin with copper and lead. The high-quality old pewter contains no lead, just tin and copper, and is a bright, silvery colour, whereas the cheap, low-quality old pewter contains a high proportion of lead and is blackish-grey in colour.

Modern pewter should really be called Britannia metal and is a tarnish-resistant mixture of tin and antimony.

Handling

See p.12. Always wear vinyl, latex, or nitrile gloves when handling lead or pewter objects rather than cotton gloves, as lead is toxic.

Display & Storage

Lead and pewter objects should not be kept in a closed space, such as a box or cupboard, made of materials that produce organic acids, such as MDF, wood, cardboard (see Problems, above): instead use archival-quality boxes or sealed plastic boxes.

Lead containers for outside plants can sag and distort if placed on blocks, so gravel is often used for support. A smooth bed of flat stones such as paving stones also works well; the gaps between the stones must be small enough (about 2cm/½in) to prevent the metal from sagging while allowing the water to run away.

Housekeeping & Maintenance

For general housekeeping, flick off the dust with a soft brush and hold the nozzle of a vacuum cleaner in the other hand to catch the dust (*see* p.14). This will prevent the dust from being spread around and will also remove any lead powder. Use a microfibre cloth or soft, lint-free cloth to dust the flat surfaces.

Wash outdoor sculpture at least once a year using a soft bristle brush and water containing a conservation-grade detergent. Brush gently to remove grime and bird droppings. Do not apply a wax coating or other protective coating as these can damage the object.

If your object is splitting or has severe corrosion, seek advice from a metal conservator.

Cleaning

A grimy lead object can be cleaned by wiping the surface with cotton swabs dampened with warm water containing a few drops of conservation-grade detergent. Rinse well with a clean swab dampened with clean water and dry with a soft clean cloth. If this is not successful, try using the water/acetone mixture (*see* solvent mixtures) on a cotton wool swab.

Pewter should have a slightly more polished appearance than lead. With pewter what you are aiming for is a dull gleam rather than a high polish. If your pewter is looking lifeless, try rubbing the surface gently with a soft cloth. If this is unsuccessful, use a fine abrasive paste on a soft cloth and gently polish the surface using a circular movement, then wipe the polish

metals

off with another clean, soft cloth. Remove any remaining polish with a cotton wool swab or soft cloth dampened with white spirit. Do not press hard, as the metal may dent. This process should be carried out infrequently, as it will wear away the metal surface.

Take care not to remove the surface patina on lead and pewter and do not remove any warts or lumps of corrosion, as you can never know what you are taking off with it. Whitish powder growing on your object is a sign of lead corrosion, so seek conservation advice if you spot this.

SILVER

Silver is a soft, white, precious metal that has been used since antiquity. It is seldom used on its own and is usually alloyed with copper.

English **sterling silver** contains about 92.5% silver with copper.

Britannia silver is 95.8% silver with copper.

Electrum is 25–40 % silver to 75–60% gold.

Silver can be applied as a thin coat to a base metal, ceramic or glass and can also be beaten into silver leaf and used to decorate picture frames, leather hangings and sculptures. When silver is applied as a coating for a base metal, it is known as silver plate. There are various forms of silver plate, including Sheffield plate, electroplate and silver plate.

Problems

- Silver objects are often dented, scratched and split from use and the surface may be worn from vigorous polishing.
- Seams can split.
- Archaeological silver often has a purplish, waxy corrosion.
- Green copper corrosion products are often found on silver that has been kept in damp conditions. This corrosion comes from the copper in the alloy, or from the base metal of coated objects. The copper will also corrode if the object is exposed to organic acid vapours.
- Hinged lids of tea and coffee pots and other vessels can be damaged if the object is left to drain upside down with the lid open. The hinge cannot take the weight of the object and may be torn out.
- Silver will tarnish eventually forming a black surface.

Sometimes the base metal is silver coloured, making it difficult to tell when the silver is worn away. In addition, the layer of silver is often very thin and easily polished off.

Ideally, store silver wrapped in bags, wraps and rolls made from good-quality cotton or silver protection cloth. If this is not possible, wrap your silver in acid-free tissue. Plastic bags made with a tarnish inhibitor are available for small objects such as coins and medals.

metals

Housekeeping & Maintenance

Remove dust with a soft brush. Use a metal polishing cloth suitable for use with silver to lightly buff up an object. A soft linen cloth or microfibre cloth can also be used, but these are not quite as effective. Dust lacquered objects with a soft brush.

Cleaning

Wash and carefully dry mustard pots, salt cellars, silver cutlery and other silver vessels as soon as possible because many foods will tarnish the silver or cause corrosion.

When tarnish is polished off, a small amount of silver is removed and the silver will eventually wear away. Similarly, silver plate can wear off and leave the base metal exposed, and engraved designs or finely textured surface decoration can be lost. It is therefore important to keep the silver in conditions that do not cause tarnish and so cut down on the need for polishing; to use materials that will help protect the silver from tarnish; and to use cleaning materials that are as non-abrasive as possible.

Prepare the table by covering it, including the edges, with a soft towel or blanket. You can also put a layer of polythene over the padding if you like. Wear vinyl, latex or nitrile gloves.

Before cleaning, check for:

* surface decoration, niello decoration and deliberate colouring, as these are easily removed by cleaning;
* tears, breaks and broken pieces, so that you do not catch them accidentally with the polishing cloth;
* very thin silver, which can be distorted if not supported while cleaning;
* a lacquer coating the surface.

Once you have checked the surface of your silver:

1 Remove dust with a soft brush.
2 Remove any greasy grime with warm water containing a few drops of conservation-grade detergent. Rinse in warm water and dry with a soft lint-free cloth or old tea towel.
3 Polish lightly tarnished silver with a silver metal polishing cloth.
4 Use silver foam or silver dip (*see* opposite) for removing tarnish. This is a cleaning agent with a fine abrasive and is supplied with a sponge. If the object is solid silver and can be washed, follow the manufacturer's instructions carefully, taking care to remove all the polish.
5 Dry and polish the silver with a soft cloth.

> ### Silver myths
> *Many traditional household tips are reliable and true, but the tradition of wrapping silver in wool baize is not recommended, as it can encourage tarnish on silver and other polished metals. Cotton baize or cloth is more suitable.*

Silver polish is not recommended for general or regular cleaning because it is abrasive and difficult to remove from crevices and decoration.

Silver dip contains chemicals that remove silver tarnish and is very useful for cleaning cutlery. It is essential that silver dip is washed off well and that none remains on the object, otherwise it will tarnish even more rapidly than usual. The manufacturers suggest that you dip your cutlery into the jar of silver dip, but it is safer to decant some of the dip into a glass jar, use it for your objects and then discard it, as old silver dip can be harmful to antique silver. Silver dip can also be used to clean larger objects but, again, it is essential that it is used only on objects that can be washed, as the silver dip needs to be washed off with warm soapy water.

CLEANING OBJECTS WITH SILVER DIP

1 Decant a little silver dip into a plastic or glass container.
2 Dampen a cotton wool bud with silver dip.
3 Wipe the surface with the damp bud and immediately rinse with warm water on a cotton swab.

4 Wash the entire object in warm water containing a little detergent.

5 Rinse in clean water.

6 Pat dry and then allow to dry thoroughly before storing.

If the object is small, you may be able to clean the whole surface with silver dip in one go, before rinsing. With larger objects, this is tricky, as the silver drip dries and can tarnish or change the surface. So work in one area at a time, cleaning with the dip and then rinsing with the damp cotton wool swab. Once the entire object is cleaned, it must be carefully washed in warm water containing a small amount of conservation-grade detergent. Rinse in clean water.

Silver that cannot be washed

Some silver objects cannot be washed or get very wet before corrosion, deterioration or staining sets in. These include objects with hollow areas such as feet, handles or rims, where water or cleaning solutions may gather; objects that have plaster- or wood-filled insides, such as candlesticks, knife handles, bases of wine coolers, large jugs, cigarette boxes etc.; and items that contain silver combined with other materials, such as wood, ivory, jewels and enamel. Never clean these items in the dishwasher or hot water – use silver foam on a cotton wool bud and use damp cotton wool swabs to rinse off the polish. Take care not to get polish on any other materials. Dry carefully.

DECORATED OBJECTS AND SILVER ENAMEL

Silver is often decorated with gemstones, enamel or other applied decoration. A silver polishing cloth and/or soft pencil eraser will usually remove most of the tarnish and will not abrade the surface. Do not use silver foam, silver dip or other liquids, as they may run under the enamel or stones and will discolour and damage the decoration.

A soft eraser and/or a silver metal polishing cloth is also very useful for cleaning the highlights on a heavily embossed or engraved object, and objects decorated with niello.

ACCUMULATED POLISH AND DIRT

Polish and dirt often accumulate in the depths and crevices of highly decorated pieces. Sometimes this enhances the decoration, but it may also obscure it. If you want to remove the accumulation, use a swab stick with a few fibres of cotton wool wrapped around it. Apply a small amount of silver foam and gently rub the surface. Clean with cotton wool dampened with warm water. Do not use a metal point as it will scratch the silver.

ELECTROCHEMICAL CLEANING

Many companies advertise an electrochemical method of cleaning silver. This process can remove more silver than is necessary and can be damaging. And with the modern cleaning materials available, you really don't need to take this course.

Protection

Silver which is on display and not used for any particular purpose in the home can be protected from tarnish by applying a coat of clear lacquer. Application of the lacquer should be carried out by an experienced metal conservator – if not done well, the silver can look unattractive and the lacquer prove ineffective.

Repair

Silver objects should be repaired by a qualified silversmith or metal conservator. Silver solder should be used rather than lead solder, which will run on the surface and is impossible to remove.

TIN AND TINPLATE

Tin is a soft, stable white metal. It is sometimes used on its own – for example, to make buttons, mugs and plates – but is more commonly used as a constituent for an alloy or as a coating, as it does not corrode very much. Iron is coated with tin (tinplate) to protect it from rust while copper and copper alloy cooking vessels are coated with tin to prevent food from reacting with the copper and producing poisonous compounds. In antiquity, tin was used to coat bronze in order to make jewellery.

Tin forms a thin protective layer on the metal it coats. Tinplated objects are often painted or have a coloured finish, sometimes decorated with gilding. Careful handling and washing are required, therefore, so that neither the protective coating, paint nor decoration become damaged.

Housekeeping & Maintenance

Remove dust with a soft brush or dry microfibre cloth. Avoid polishing the surface, as it will remove the protective tin layer.

Cleaning

Tinplate is often very dirty, but it is preferable to keep it dry to avoid the risk of removing paint or decoration, or of encouraging iron corrosion. For small spots of dirt and grime, saliva on a cotton bud should do the trick. Tin objects that are in good condition and are very grimy can be washed – use warm water containing a few drops of conservation-grade detergent. Rinse with clean water and dry with a soft cloth. Leave in a warm place overnight to ensure the items are thoroughly dry before putting away.

If the surface of your object seems sound, try cleaning it with a dry chemical sponge. If this is unsuccessful wipe the surface carefully with cotton swabs or buds dampened with water containing a few drops of conservation-grade detergent. Check first that the paint does not come off by testing over a small inconspicuous area. If you see colour on the cotton wool, do not proceed. Rinse with clean swabs of cotton wool dampened with water.

An alternative method of cleaning would be to try the water/white spirit detergent solution (*see* solvent mixtures) on a cotton bud. Again, check that the cleaning solution does not take the paint off first.

It is essential to dry the object thoroughly with paper towels or soft cloth and to make sure you do not leave water sitting in crevices or corners.

Leave to stand in a warm place overnight to ensure that the object is completely dry.

Wax the surface thoroughly with microcrystalline wax applied with a soft brush and polish with soft lint-free cloth. Test on a small area first to ensure the wax does not remove the paint.

Textiles
& Carpets

Textiles include fabrics made by weaving, crocheting, knitting, lace-making, braiding, knotting (carpets) and embroidery, as well as non-woven materials such as felt. There are three groups of fibres used to make textiles:

Plant fibres, such as cotton and linen
Animal-derived fibres, such as wool and silk
Synthetic fibres

Textiles tend to be known as three-dimensional – for example clothing, uniforms, hats etc. – or two-dimensional – for example, carpets, bedspreads, tablecloths, shawls or veils.

Problems
Light and insects are the main enemies of textiles, as well as dirt, mould, poor repair, handling and packing. The secret to caring for your textiles, therefore, is to minimise exposure to light, dirt and damp and to prevent attack from insects, mice or other pests.

LIGHT
Visible and ultraviolet light fades colours and weakens fibres. This is often most noticeable in curtain linings, which can split. You can easily see how

light has affected your fabric by comparing the front with a hidden area such as the back or a seam. A faded textile means a weakened textile, and it will therefore need particularly careful handling. Closing blinds/shutters or curtains when the room is not in use helps reduce light damage.

INSECTS

Insects, particularly the larvae of some types of moth and carpet beetle, as well as silverfish and cockroaches, can damage textiles. The materials most at risk are wool, silk, fur, feathers and other animal-derived textiles. Old food, stains, body fluids, dirt and dust attract moths and beetles – insects rarely attack clean fabrics. Look for signs in clothes in areas like under

Spotting insect damage

Moth – small irregular holes, sometimes white cocoon wisps, larvae cases and frass that is the same colour as the textile.

Carpet beetle – small, neat holes that are more widely spread than moth, surface grazing, no frass. The cases of pupae, known as woolly bears, can often be found nearby.

Silverfish – surface grazing, seldom form holes.

arms, pockets, collars, front of shirts, crotches of trousers and turn-ups. Keeping storage and display areas clean and dust free is the most important aspect of insect control.

DIRT

Dust and grit can cause minute cuts in the fibres; for example, walking on a dirty carpet will cause the carpet to wear faster than walking on a clean carpet. Pollution, particularly acid from wood or cardboard, may weaken or discolour threads. Cleaning textiles exposes them to extra physical wear and tear, so prevent them from getting too dirty so that cleaning can be kept to a minimum. Residues of soap and detergent can cause white fabrics to yellow.

MOULD

Mould, which may stain and weaken the fabric, can develop in damp basements and other damp areas; in objects stored in polythene bags as a result of condensation in the bag; and in framed items hung on an outside wall without circulation behind the frame. Damp in stone, terracotta or brick floors can be enough for mould to appear under carpets and rugs.

ACCESSORIES

Metal pins, jewellery, buttons and other fastenings may stain and weaken the textile, so any extraneous accessories should be removed.

Handling

Always have clean hands and make sure that any surface you lay the textile on is clean and dry, preferably covered in a clean dustsheet.

Underlay

All carpets need some sort of underlay to cushion them from the unevenness of the floor and so minimise wear. The best underlay is natural fibre felt. It should come to the edge, or even beyond the edge, of the carpet and should, ideally, be made from one piece. If more than one piece has to be used, the pieces must be sewn together so that they butt each other but do not overlap. Trim the underlay with scissors to match any irregular shape of the rug and trim again when necessary, as the underlay will spread with time. Use a non-adhesive anti-creep tape or mat on the underside of the underfelt on slippery floors or use non-slip underlay under the ordinary underlay.

Display

In a perfect world, all two-dimensional textiles would be displayed in glazed frames or, even better, in cases where they can be kept flat. Of course, this is not always practical; often we want to display our textiles on the wall. Yet hanging textiles in this way can cause them to weaken and break, particularly if the display system does not support the full width of

the textile, so follow the advice on Hanging and seek conservation advice for particularly fragile pieces.

Textiles can be badly damaged by metal fixings, so avoid securing a textile with pins, drawing pins, tacks, wire staples or other metal fixings.

Small carpets or other large, strong, two-dimensional textiles can be hung from a support (*see* opposite) but smaller items, including antique embroideries and samplers, are better protected when mounted on a cloth-covered board. Sometimes stretcher frames are used for this purpose, but this puts too much strain on the fabric and the centre is not supported. It also means that dirt can penetrate from both sides.

Carpets and rugs have to cope with heavy traffic, so carry the greatest risk of damage. To minimise wear:

- Move rugs and carpets around to prevent one area from receiving more light than another, and to spread the wear.

- Make sure that a carpet lies flat on the floor, otherwise the top of any wrinkles will begin to be worn bare.

- If your carpet is on a stone floor and there is no damp-proof course, use a heavy-duty damp-proof paper, available from carpet shops, between the floor and the underlay to protect the carpet from rising damp. It is also advisable to use the same paper on a wood floor, to act as a barrier for the dust that rises between the floorboards.

- A carpet placed on top of a larger or fitted carpet will have a tendency to 'walk' in the direction of the pile of the fitted carpet. To prevent this, sew a heavy canvas, slightly smaller than the top carpet, to the fitted carpet.

HANGING A CARPET OR STRONG, TWO-DIMENSIONAL TEXTILE

A carpet or other strong, large textile in good condition can be hung vertically by supporting it along the full length of its upper edge. This can be done using a hook and loop fastener.

You will need:

◊ a wooden batten the width of the carpet;
◊ a hook and loop fastener 5cm (2in) wide and of a length to match the carpet width;
◊ cotton webbing of a length to match the carpet width;
◊ buttonhole thread;
◊ a straight needle.

1 Firmly fix the batten to the wall.
2 Sew the soft half, or loop side, of the fastener to the cotton webbing.

3 Stab stitch (*see* box, p66) both edges of the webbing to the carpet about 1.5cm (⅝in) from the top.
4 Fix the hook side of the fastener to the wooden batten with staples.
5 Press the two halves of the tape together. Arrange the top of the carpet so that the carpet hangs flat and straight.

Storage

Ideally textiles should be stored so that they are protected from light, dust, damp, insects and pollution and are padded, rolled or hung in a way that helps prevent creases from forming but supports the textile.

Before putting items away, you should clean them or have them cleaned. Remove metal pins, brooches, staples or metal fastenings and trimmings as is feasible. If you cannot remove these accessories, slip some acid-free tissue or card between the fitting, such as a button, and the textile. You will need to slit the card so that it will go under the entire button.

Textiles are protected from light and dust by being folded and stored in drawers or, preferably, in acid-free or archival-quality boxes. The boxes should have lids and be big enough to prevent the textile from being squashed. Line the drawer or box with plenty of tissue paper and use wads of acid-free tissue to pad the folds and creases. Shoes, bags, hats, umbrellas and other items can also be padded into the correct shape and stored in acid-free boxes. Try as far as possible not to keep clothes or other costumes on hangers, as the weight of the textile can cause them to split or break up.

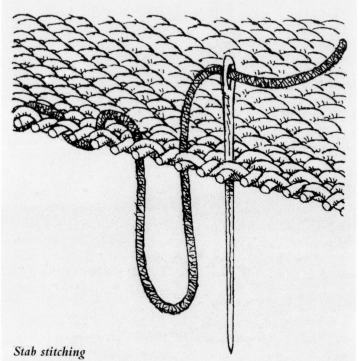

Stab stitching

A stab stitch is a short running stitch made by sewing straight down through the textile, between the threads, and straight up a little further along. Take care not to split the yarns by stitching through them – the needle must pass between the warps and the wefts. Each stitch should cross about 2 warps. The pile will hide the stitches.

ROLLING A TEXTILE

Flat textiles such as shawls, sashes, tablecloths or wedding veils benefit from being rolled rather than folded, as squashed folds become creases that will, in time, crack and tear. Carpets and rugs should also be rolled where practicable. You will need:

- acid-free card tube with a diameter not less than 5cm (2in) for smaller objects, 10–12cm (4–5in) for medium-sized objects; and 20–30cm (8–12in), for larger and/or stiffer objects. (N.B. these tubes are seldom acid-free. PVC tubes or drainpipes or the cardboard tubes designed for commercial carpets are useful for larger textiles. The tube must be longer than the width of the object being rolled so there is at least 5cm (2in) of the tube protruding beyond the edge of the textile. Carpets and large objects need a wider margin, as they are seldom perfectly square and straight;
- brackets from which to suspend the roll;
- a metal pole to go through the tube; the pole is suspended from the brackets;
- aluminium foil or clear polyester film;
- acid-free tissue.

1 If the tube is not acid-free, cover it with aluminium foil or clear polyester film and then wrap the tube in several layers of acid-free tissue. Make sure that the tissue is smooth and firm around the tube.

2 Lay the textile face down on a clean, flat surface – all items are rolled with the right side outwards. You'll need an extra pair of hands to roll large items.

3 If the textile has a pile, it must be rolled in the direction of the pile. To establish this, move your hand on the surface of the carpet towards both ends. The direction in which the pile feels smoother is the direction of the pile.

4 Woven items should be rolled in the direction of the warp so that the weft threads are parallel to the tube.

5 Cover the reverse side of the object with acid-free tissue.

6 Place the tube at the end of the textile and bring the fabric around the tube, then roll the textile around the tube, keeping the fabric tight and smooth. Smooth out any creases and folds as you go.

7 Cover the roll with acid-free tissue, washed calico, Tyvek or an old, clean sheet.

8 Secure the cover with 5-cm (2-in) wide strips of white cotton tape or hook and loop fastener.

9 Suspend the roll by pushing the pole through the tube and resting the end of the pole on the brackets.

Small rolled items without a pile can be placed in drawers or boxes, but it is always better to suspend them where possible. They can also be rolled round tubes of scrunched acid-free tissue. To do this, take a piece of tissue slightly larger than the item to be rolled, and scrunch it up as you are making the roll, so the surface is not smooth. Then take another similar piece of tissue and roll this smoothly around the scrunched-up roll. This will make a more stable covering for small textiles. Make sure you don't squash items in a drawer or have any other items placed on top of them.

Housekeeping & Maintenance

Fragile and precious textiles can be easily damaged by cleaning and so should only be cleaned by a textile conservator. Cleaning is carried out frequently enough to keep the dirt and dust at bay but not so often that the risk of damage is increased.

Precious textiles in good condition, such as a delicate bedspread, upholstery or a sampler, can be cleaned with a vacuum cleaner crevice tool protected by netting. Use a vacuum that allows control of the strength of suction.

1 Cover the end of the crevice tool with nylon net and hold it in place with an elastic band around the crevice tool. This is to prevent tassels, fringes, loose threads or the textile itself being sucked into the vacuum cleaner.
2 Lightly brush or pat the object to loosen the dirt before vacuuming.
3 Gently move the crevice tool just above the surface of the textile (about 5mm/¼in) and take care not to rub the nozzle on the fabric.
4 Hold the nozzle at a 45° angle so that you can see the area being vacuumed.

5 Gently move the crevice tool across the textile, making sure you go over the entire surface.

It can be easier to clean a large object such as a bedspread by using a square of mesh rather than covering the end of the vacuum cleaner with net. Use plastic fly screening and cut out a piece about 30cm (1ft) square then bind the edges by sewing white cotton tape over them. Place the net on the surface of the object and use a flat upholstery tool to vacuum through the net. This square of net can also be used to clean small objects such as samplers or lace. In this case the net should be laid over the object and pinned in place around, not to, the textile.

CLEANING A RUG

An antique rug should be cleaned as necessary but not as often as a new carpet.

- Use a smooth nozzle and put the vacuum cleaner on a low setting. Do not use an upright vacuum cleaner or a head with rotating brushes, as these can beat the fibres.

- If the rug is very dirty or placed in a high traffic area, cleaning is more efficient if the dirt is first loosened by 'tamping'. To do this, turn the rug upside down and pat the reverse with the flat of your hand or a large, flexible rubber paddle. The dust that comes out can be vacuumed up.
- Vacuum the rug in the direction of the pile, not against or across it. You can occasionally vacuum against the pile if the rug is very dirty, but this should not be regular practice.
- Occasionally vacuum under a rug on its reverse.
- Use net over the nozzle or a net square when vacuuming old, worn or frayed areas.
- Use doormats at entrances to catch dust and dirt and vacuum these regularly.

! Silk carpets wear very easily and so should not be vacuumed too vigorously.

PREVENTION AND TREATMENT FOR INSECTS

Good housekeeping is the best way to prevent insects from taking hold of your textiles. Clean dark and hidden areas such as heating ducts, cupboards, cellars and attics, boxed-in radiators, the edges of fitted carpets and under furniture at least annually. Clean more accessible places more frequently.

Insect inhibitors such as mothballs (naphthalene) and radichlorobenzene do repel adult clothes moths and carpet beetles but only in high concentrations. The health and safety aspects of these chemicals is under review and their use with textiles is no longer recommended. So why not try some natural alternatives.

Natural insect repellents

Evidence suggests that, in high doses, lavender and cedarwood oil are reasonably effective insect repellents. And, of course, they smell much nicer than chemical ones! You can spray lavender oil onto shelves, around windows and in drawers, but don't spray on the textile directly; instead use lavender bags and bunches of dried lavender. Spraying these areas will also deter flies and some other insects. Herbs that have traditionally been used to protect textiles include mint, sage, rosemary, bay, mugwort, thyme, santolina, sothernwood, woodruff and sweet marjoram, either used individually or mixed together. Make your own muslin sachets to put in wardrobes, drawers and storage boxes or buy sachets of herbs that are specifically sold as insect deterrents. It is not safe, however, to assume that these methods will totally protect your textiles.

Insecticides based on permethrin have been developed for historic collections and are also available commercially. The solution is spayed onto shelves, floors and storage material but not directly onto antique textiles.

If you think you have insects (*see* box, p.60, Spotting Insect Damage) follow these steps:

- Isolate the objects in question and seal them in a polyethylene bag until you can deal with them (but do not leave them in the bag for any longer than 2 months).
- Carefully vacuum the cupboard and shelves where the objects were kept to remove all dust, eggs and larvae.
- Spray the shelves with permethrin (or lavender if you prefer).
- Ideally, take your object in its bag outside so that insect eggs are not scattered in the house, and carefully vacuum off all the debris and larvae.
- Thoroughly wash the vacuum cleaner nozzle and throw away the vacuum bag and net.
- If the item can withstand washing, try to have it wet or dry cleaned (*see* below).

Cleaning

Textiles may need more than mere vacuuming, particularly when newly acquired, or before putting them into store. Too much cleaning can weaken the threads or change the dyes, so wherever possible, get advice from a textile conservator before embarking on a cleaning project. Commercial carpet cleaners, carpet shampoo and machines that generate steam can also cause dyes to run and are best avoided.

There are two types of washing:

Wet cleaning   – with water
Dry cleaning   – in cleaning solvent

Strong fibres can be wet cleaned if the dyes are colour fast, there are no metal threads and the construction of the textiles is suitable. Most types of fabric can be solvent cleaned.

DRY CLEANING
The advantages of solvent or dry cleaning are:

* special finishes such as glazed chintzes are not affected
* few dyes will run
* the solvents are less harmful than water to pile fabrics such as velvets
* pleats and tucks set in with heat and steam are not removed

If you are in doubt about whether a piece can be washed or dry cleaned, consult a textile conservator and certainly ask about fragile, rare or ancient textiles. If possible, use a specialist firm that has some interest in and experience of cleaning old textiles (a local museum may be able to advise you) and don't be afraid to ask questions. Try to find a dry-cleaning firm where the drum does not rotate (this is too vigorous) but moves gently back and forth and that uses clean solvent.

WET CLEANING

Although wet cleaning can help the preservation of textiles, it is difficult to judge whether threads and dyes will be enhanced or damaged. It is also hard to assess whether the structure of a costume will hold up to being washed. Textile conservators always carry out extensive tests on objects before cleaning them and it is not possible here to discuss all the dangers of wet cleaning. The advice, therefore, is to clean white cotton and linen only. Simple cotton christening gowns or night dresses, cotton covers, household linens and lace can usually be washed safely, provided you follow these instructions:

- Remove as much dust and loose dirt as possible by vacuuming prior to washing
- Never machine wash
- Use purified, distilled or deionised water
- Never use bleach, as it weakens the fabric
- Wherever possible, remove the lining and wash it separately

You will need:

◊ a large, shallow, plastic container such as are sold in garden centres and photographic shops. Use a bath for larger objects;

◊ plenty of purified, distilled or deionised water, cold or lukewarm;

◊ a liquid conservation-grade detergent;

◊ nylon net – such as nylon fly screen, cut to provide a piece larger than the size of the textile;

◊ sponges;

◊ a clean flat surface;

◊ white towels;

◊ a smooth surface such as a sheet of glass, Formica, board covered with polyethylene or clear polyester film.

Washing

1 Pour enough water into the container to easily cover the object, and so the dirt can float out.

2 Add a few drops of the detergent.

3 Place the textile on the net and lower it carefully into the water.

4 Gently submerge the textile.

5 Dab the textile with the sponge. Press and release the sponge along the whole length of the textile. Do not squeeze or rub with your hands.

6 When the whole textile has been washed, lift it out on the nylon net by holding both ends of the net.

7 Tip the water away and if the textile was very dirty wash it again.

Rinsing

1 Pour clean water into the container.

2 Put the object into the water on the net and wash with a clean, detergent-free sponge, using the same method as for washing.

3 Remove the object on the net before discarding the water.

4 Rinse two or three times and remove all traces of the detergent.

5 Lay the net and the textile on a clean, white bath towel, lay another towel on top and press down gently to absorb the excess water.

6 Lay the textile flat on a smooth surface with the right side facing upwards and smooth it into shape while damp.

7 Dry naturally, away from sunlight and artificial heat. Good ventilation speeds up drying, so an electric fan that is not heated may help.

Any stains and spots that remain after cleaning are best left alone. In general, more harm is done by trying to remove them.

Textiles that should never be washed

Silk or satin banners, flags and tapestries, silk or satin embroideries, or textiles which show any sign that the base fabric has weak areas, should never be washed. The same goes for textiles that are light damaged, have metal threads, metal fastenings or decoration, or have been repaired. These should be cleaned by a textile conservator.

IRONING

Heat and moisture accelerate decay, so very old or fragile textiles should not be ironed. The best advice is to iron only cotton or linen objects in good condition. Try to arrange the wet textiles so they dry flat and never iron a textile that has not been cleaned, as the heat fixes many stains and seals in dust and dirt. Use a lightweight iron on its lowest setting, with a pressing rather than a rubbing action. Often just hanging your fabric in a steamy bathroom will make the creases drop out of wool, silk or velvet. Pile fabrics such as velvet should be ironed as little as possible. If you do have to, iron it on the back with the pile lying against another piece of velvet.

STARCH

Insects love starch, so it's best to steer clear of it. Starch also makes your fabrics brittle and can easily crack. Old-fashioned starch, which is in fact rice starch, can be used for christening dresses or wedding veils but be sure to always wash the starch out before storing them again. Never use spray-on stiffeners or plastic starch, as these are difficult to wash out.

SPILLS

If you spill liquid on a carpet, mop it up using a dry cloth or paper towel.

1 Put the paper towel over the spill and press it with your hands.
2 Replace the towel when the first one is damp.
3 Continue until no more liquid is absorbed.

If you spill a liquid that might stain, such as tea, coffee or wine, mop up as much as possible with towels, then dampen the area with a little soda water or tap water and continue the mopping.

Repair

Repairing textiles is a difficult and skilled job. Rare and precious items should always be repaired by a textile conservator, who will strengthen torn and weak fabrics by carefully sewing them onto a suitable backing material.

Removing red wine stains

Most of us will have heard a story about how to deal with red wine spills – pouring salt, soda water or white wine on the stain being the most common. But the most effective method is to simply mop up as much of the wine as possible using paper towels. Do not rub the stain but press on the towels – you can stand on them if you want – then pour over a little water (soda water will do). Repeat the process until the stain has disappeared.

Salt does absorb the liquid but scientific opinion states that salt can in fact make the stain harder to remove. Not surprising, given that it is often used as a fixative for dyes.

Furniture

Most of the furniture in your home will be made of wood, though you may well have leather sofas, plastic, cane or bamboo chairs, textiles for upholstery, or items made of metal, ivory, stone, etc.

Furniture may be decorated in a number of ways:

- gilded, painted, lacquered or japanned
- inlaid with metals, shell, ivory, bone or wood
- decorated with mirrors, ceramic, glass, metal or tortoiseshell

Veneer was first used in Europe in the mid-seventeenth century and is a thin section of timber that is sawn or sliced off the tree trunk and applied in sheets to the furniture carcass.

Marquetry is made from veneers with varying colours and patterns, cut to form floral or figurative scenes, and applied to the furniture carcass. Sometimes other materials such as bone or brass are included.

Parquetry is inlaid or veneered wood laid in a geometric pattern.

Wood furniture is often finished with a protective or decorative coating. A simple and common seal and finish is wax, usually beeswax, or oil. Although wax can be used on its own, traditionally an oil polish or oil varnish made with linseed oil was applied.

furniture

Problems

Most damage to furniture is from wear and tear – joints become weak, knobs and other fittings become loose and surfaces get scratched and bruised. The following problems may also occur.

* Wood will shrink and swell with changes of humidity. In dry conditions it may crack, joints may open and become loose, and veneer may lift. In damp conditions the wood may swell, the glue soften and, again, the veneer may lift.
* As with most organic materials, mould will grow in damp conditions and may stain the surface. Mould is a particular problem where air circulation is poor and can grow inside cupboards, commodes and chests that are near an outside wall and not opened regularly.
* Furniture often has a complex structure and stresses occur where there is a differential between the shrinkage of the various parts, such as in panels in a chest, veneers on a wood carcass or metal fixings on timber furniture, resulting in cracks or warping.
* Paint, gilding, japanning and lacquer may flake and become loose. Other applied decoration may lift and loosen.
* Most woods change colour in light – some bleach and some darken. Light will also damage textile upholstery (*see* p.8), leather,

tortoiseshell and other organic materials as well as some plastics, paint and japanning. Light can weaken the material – the surface becomes matt and eventually may crumble.

- Spilt liquids can leave white or dark stains on some materials or wood finishes. Hot and cold objects can also mark the surface.
- Wood is prone to attack by wood-boring insects (*see* pp.92–3). Basketry, which is sometimes used to make furniture, is particularly vulnerable.
- Self-adhesive tape or labels can damage the surface if stuck onto the finished side of a piece of furniture. If a piece needs to be labelled, use tie-on labels or fix a label to the underside or unfinished area.
- The base (legs, feet, bottom rungs) of furniture can be damaged by vacuum cleaners, mops, etc. Always move chairs and lightweight furniture when vacuuming or washing the floor and clean carefully by hand around those pieces that cannot be moved.

Handling

The golden rule is to move one piece of furniture at a time and always lift by the least fragile part – ie, the lowest solid part of the main frame or body. The most vulnerable areas are the arms and legs of chairs, the top edges and legs of tables, and the feet and bases of chests and cabinets.

* Never drag furniture across the floor, even if it has castors, as dragging puts a great strain on the joints.
* Use two people to carry a piece where possible.
* Make sure belt buckles and watches won't scratch the object you are carrying.
* Lift tables and chests of drawers by the top support rail rather than by the parts that project beyond the frame or carcass, such as the overhang or rim. Empty and remove the drawers, and carry them separately.
* Do not lift chairs by their backs or arms; place your hands under the seat on each side or on the legs, taking care not to apply any pressure to the arms.
* Lock or tie doors closed before moving cupboards. Use soft webbing or tape rather than string.
* Remove marble, glass and other movable tops and carry separately. Always carry them vertically – they can break under their own weight if carried flat.

furniture

Display & Storage

Furniture should be kept at a steady humidity, ideally not below 45% rh or above 65% rh (*see* p. 9). Avoid placing pieces near radiators or in direct sunlight and where possible protect them by using blinds and curtains – light can cause furniture to develop a patchy appearance or change colour. Place a piece of brown felt or chamois leather under photographs, ceramics and other objects that are displayed on furniture – they can easily scratch the finish. Use mats to give protection from spilt drinks, condensation running down the sides of cold glasses, and hot or cold plates. If you are using a table to write on, place some card or a blotter between the paper and the table.

furniture

French polish

It is thought that French polish (shellac varnish) was first used in France in the late seventeenth century, but it was in the nineteenth century that it really became popular and widely used. In the 1930s it gave way to cellulose lacquers, as these were seen to be tougher and easier to maintain. Shellac is a natural resin produced in India and harvested from insects. The best shellac dissolved in alcohol is used to make true French polish. The shellac is applied to a surface using a lint-free 'rubber' or cotton pad and sometimes a little linseed oil is used as a lubricant. The layers of polish are built up to produce a gloss finish, which varies from a high shine to a soft lustre. A lot of furniture dating from before 1820 has now been French polished, even though it would not in fact have had such a finish originally.

DISPLAYING PLANTS AND FLOWERS

Where feasible, remove your flowers and houseplants to another area before watering. This is generally possible with houseplants, but more risky with vases of flowers.

- Place the vase or pot on a waterproof mat that is larger than the base of the vase and, ideally, big enough to catch any pollen.
- Use a long-nosed watering can and immediately mop up any water spilt

on the furniture. Make sure the water does not run under the mat and do not overfill vases. If you tuck your finger over the edge of the vase, you will feel the water when it reaches your finger tip – ie before it gets to the top and spills over!

- Never spray plants with water if they are standing on furniture.
- Make sure that the leaves or flowers of houseplants do not rest or dip on the surface of your furniture.
- Never put houseplants or vases on gilded furniture, as the smallest drop of water can completely ruin the gilding.

Housekeeping & Maintenance

Monitor the condition of your furniture regularly and deal with any problem as soon as possible. Look for:

- splitting and warping
- lifting veneers
- loose metalwork and inlay
- flaking, cracking and lifting surfaces
- loose joints, legs and stretchers

DUSTING

A flat surface in good condition should need only a light dusting. Use a clean, dry microfibre cloth or lint-free duster with hemmed edges. Microfibre cloths work well on glass and plastic furniture, but it may help

furniture

to use a very slightly damp cloth. Do not use modern cleaning products on old plastic, as the chemicals can damage the plastic. Follow the manufacturers' cleaning instructions for modern plastic furniture. Leather can be dusted with a dry microfibre cloth or duster. Modern leather furniture should be cleaned following the manufacturers' instructions. Sometimes the best cleaning method is to brush-vacuum using a ponyhair or hogshair brush. A brush is used because it is efficient and less likely to pull up, or even pull off, bits of veneer, inlay, tortoiseshell and other applied decoration that is sticking up, or flaking paint, gilding or lacquer.

Insects and mould

Check for signs of insect infestation and mould at least once a year, preferably in the spring.

Look inside drawers and cupboards, and check crevices in soft wood, all backboards, and other unfinished surfaces. Vacuum inside furniture and move furniture that is standing on carpets away from its usual position so that you can clean underneath. Don't ignore furniture that has a lining of baize, silk or leather, such as boxes, drawers, suitcases and card tables – insects can easily make a home here. Check poorly ventilated areas for mould and open doors and drawers in spare rooms to aid ventilation.

furniture

Brush-vacuum:

* carved furniture;
* delicate surfaces such as Boulle, gilding, lacquer, paint, marquetry, inlaid furniture;
* damaged surfaces such as missing or lifting veneer.

Dusters

We are all familiar with those standard yellow dusters, but they are not necessarily your best friend; they can snag on rough areas, pulling veneer or splinters away, and they often leave yellow fluff behind. Dusters also have the disadvantage of holding onto the dust, which is abrasive and can scratch delicate surfaces. Feather dusters are not recommended, as they cannot be washed and the feathers tend to break and their spines scratch the surface. Equally, long-handled fleece dusters often leave fluff on the furniture. Brushes that pick up dust using static electricity have recently become available and are a very effective alternative. A brush is also more effective in crevices and for intricate carving.

furniture

POLISHING AND WAXING

Wax polish helps protect wood furniture and maintain the patina and sheen. A mistake that many people make is to wax too much and too often. In reality, a piece of furniture that has been waxed and polished over the years may only need buffing up with a clean, soft lint-free cloth to revive the shine. You will need to wax, however, when the surface has become worn and dull and will not shine when buffed.

You will need:

◊ Beeswax polish. Try to match the colour of the polish to that of the wood. Pale yellow wax on dark wood may show white in cracks and carving detail when it dries. Dark wax on light wood will darken it and spoil the appearance;
◊ Two soft lint-free dusters;
◊ Two soft, natural bristle brushes for carved wood.

Apply a very thin layer of wax with the cloth or brush. (Don't overdo it – if a layer of wax is allowed to build up, it will turn dull and collect dust.) Allow the wax to dry and polish off with a clean cloth or brush. If you think the veneer or inlay may be lifting, apply the wax with a soft brush and carefully polish it off with a brush and cloth.

Objects that have a natural or 'raw' finish are not generally waxed. Brush away dust and wipe with a clean, damp cloth in the direction of the grain.

Aerosol polishes

These should always be avoided. The solvent in the polish can cause white marks or a bloom on the surface of the wood, and can dissolve some applied finishes. In addition, aerosol polishes do not give much protection, as they offer only a thin coating. Most contain silicone, which should not be used on anything other than modern synthetic finishes; the shine does not look good on antique furniture and the silicone can build up and is extremely difficult to remove.

French polish (*see* p.86), shellac, varnish, paint, lacquer or oil finishes should not be waxed but burnished with a soft, dry cloth. However, because furniture is something that is being regularly used, a thin coating of wax may be necessary to help protect the surface from the hazards of everyday life.

PROTECTING LEATHER

Many people believe that the condition of leather can be improved by 'feeding', so they apply leather dressings. These are generally a mixture of oils and wax, often with lanolin. However, dressings are rarely effective; the condition of leather depends on the type of the original leather, the tanning techniques and the environmental conditions, and these are things which cannot be changed or improved by a leather dressing. In fact, recent evidence suggests that the dressings themselves can be damaging. Your best bet is to wax your leather furniture with a good-quality beeswax polish, as described above. Follow the suppliers' or manufacturers' instructions for the care and maintenance of modern leather furniture.

PROTECTING AGAINST INSECT ATTACK

The main enemy of your wood and upholstery is the furniture beetle or woodworm *Anobium punctatum*. The death-watch beetle and powderpost beetle are also found.

The damage is actually caused by the beetles' larvae, which burrow into the wood in search of food and protection. The larvae can tunnel for up to five years, after which they eventually emerge from the wood as mature beetles, leaving the characteristic round 'flight holes'. Wood-boring insects do not survive well if the moisture content of the wood is low. For this reason, woodworm is rarely a problem in centrally heated houses.

Look for the tell-tale flight holes on the backs and undersides of furniture, particularly softwood backboards, and in divisions on cupboards and mirrors. Holes in the wood do not necessarily indicate active woodworm – it depends whether they are new or old holes. New flight holes are usually a sign of insects. They are clean and the edges of the holes are crisp. With old flight holes, the edges have darkened and are less sharp.

You might find small piles of frass by a flight hole, but this does not necessarily mean the hole is new, as the frass could be old but recently shaken out. If you suspect you may have an insect infestation, carry out a test by filling the holes with a coloured wax. If new flight holes appear, you know that you need to treat the furniture.

The methods of treating furniture for insects have changed over recent years because of a greater awareness of the potential harm to humans and objects of many traditional insecticides. Today, museums or historic houses tend to avoid insecticides altogether, but you can use permethrin-based liquid insecticides, as long as you are careful not to use them on painted, lacquered, gilded or upholstered furniture, or old, rare and precious pieces. For best results:

- Take the furniture outside or into a garage or outhouse or, if this is not possible, ensure you work in a well-ventilated room. Do not keep the treated furniture in a room that is used a lot – you'll need plenty of time to allow the volatile materials to disappear.
- Remove and empty cupboards and drawers, etc.
- Dust and clean the object well first, including the inside.
- Follow the manufacturers' instructions and note the health and safety advice provided.
- Do not apply the insecticide to the finished surface (wax, French polish, etc.) but rather to the unfinished areas such as inside the drawers and carcass. Ensure the insecticide does not run onto the finished surface.

furniture

Cleaning

Occasionally furniture needs a more thorough clean than just a dust and polish. Always test in an inconspicuous spot first, as cleaning solutions can easily damage the finish or the main construction material. Gilded, painted and Boulle furniture, and furniture with a special finish or in poor condition, should be cleaned by, or with the advice of, a furniture conservator. The same goes for very old and valuable pieces. Always dust or brush-vacuum the object first to remove any loose dirt.

With wood it is best to remove grime and dirt without getting the surface wet, so first try cleaning with a dry chemical sponge, which can be used on any sound surface. Cut a handy-sized piece of sponge off the main block with scissors or a scalpel, and pull it along the surface in lines, in one direction only. Do not rub it back and forth. If the process is effective, you will see dirt being absorbed. When the sponge gets dirty, use a new piece, and if it is pulling up pieces of the surface, stop.

If the chemical sponge method is not strong enough to remove all the dirt, you may have more success with a carefully applied washing solution of deionised or purified water mixed with a few drops of conservation-grade detergent.

1 Wipe the surface with a cotton wool swab barely dampened with the cleaning solution. Replace the swab with a new one as soon as it is dirty.
2 Concentrate on one area of the wood and clean the whole of that area thoroughly before moving on to a new area. If you let the dirt dry on

one area and return to it later, it will simply be more difficult to remove. Having said that, you will need to use your own judgement: if you over-clean the surface, it can end up looking blotchy, with some areas much cleaner than others.

3 Use cotton wool buds to clean intricate areas.

4 Rinse with swabs dampened with clean water and dry the surface with a soft cloth or paper towel.

5 Do not allow the surface to get very wet, as it may stain or discolour. If you see any change in the surface appearance, stop cleaning and allow the object to dry. Then seek conservation advice.

6 Do not let any metal fittings get wet, as they may corrode.

Wax often gathers in carvings and crevices and can be removed by scraping carefully with a bamboo stick or a plastic spatula. Solvents such as white spirit can damage the surrounding surface before they soften the encrusted sections and should therefore be avoided.

Repair

Signs of structural damage to furniture such as loose legs, chair rails, slats, etc. can become serious if repairs are neglected. However, to successfully carry out such repairs demands a good understanding of the structure of furniture. Temporary repairs or a badly executed repair can exacerbate the problem and reduce the piece's value, so it is always wise to take the advice of an experienced furniture conservator.

furniture

DEALING WITH MINOR REPAIRS

Small pieces of veneer, marquetry and inlay can be glued back on without too much difficulty. You will need:

◊ a scalpel or sharp chisel;
◊ easily reversible adhesive;
◊ a clamp or weight;
◊ some small, flat blocks of wood or hardboard to prevent the clamp or weight from marking the surface;
◊ a sheet of silicone paper to prevent the blocks from sticking to the object.

1 Carefully clean off the old glue from the carcass and the back of the loose piece with a scalpel or chisel.
2 Place a small amount of adhesive in the space to be taken by the veneer.
3 Take care not to use too much otherwise it will ooze out.
4 Adjust the piece of veneer into position.
5 Place the silicone paper over the repair and place the flat block on top of the silicone paper.
6 Clamp the paper and block in position using a G-clamp or wood clamp or use a weight on top of the block.
7 Leave the adhesive to dry for about 24 hours.

Masking tape can be used to hold the piece in position while the adhesive dries but only where it will not damage the surface when it is removed. Do not use masking tape on painted, gilded or lacquered surfaces, or on any loose or flaking surface.

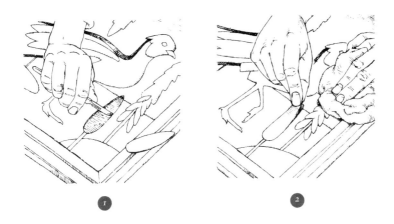

Paper, Prints
& Drawings

Paper can be made from a number of different materials, including rags, hemp, wood bark, maize and wood pulp. It is sized or finished with substances such as gelatine so that it can be written or drawn on. This chapter covers books, prints, photographs and other objects that have paper as their base.

European papers were made from cotton or linen rags until the nineteenth century, when wood pulp began to be used as well. This change was significant – wood pulp paper contains materials that may decompose to form acids, so it is less durable than rag paper. Just look at how quickly a newspaper will start to change colour and texture if you leave it lying around for a few days.

We usually think of paper as the base material for drawings, writing, photographs, books and magazines, maps and posters, as well as ephemera such as cigarette cards and tickets, but it is also used for three-dimensional objects such as fans, models, screens, lampshades and even furniture.

The 'text block' of books is usually made up of pages made of paper, but before about the fourteenth century the text block was usually vellum, and even today special editions are made from silk, bark or other materials. The Western-style book, known as the codex book, is comprised of pages – known as leaves – that have been sewn or glued together, then attached to boards (the cover) for protection. A range of materials is used for the cover, including strawboard, paper, leather, wood fabric and synthetic materials.

Problems

Paper is a delicate material and is easily damaged by the environment and by handling, as are paints, inks, photographic media and other materials found on the surface of paper. Books are particularly delicate. Paper objects are difficult to clean and so it is best to keep them framed or boxed.

- Light makes paper fibres brittle and changes the colour of inks, paints, photographic images and chalks. High temperatures increase the rate of damage by light.
- Mould will grow if there is damp or poor ventilation. Mould will also grow on photographic gelatine, binding media and other materials on the paper.
- Low humidity makes paper brittle and may cause paint or photographs to crack. Fluctuating humidity weakens paper.
- Iron gall ink is acidic and can destroy paper, leaving it in a lace-like condition.
- Inappropriate mounting and cleaning can cause physical damage and may pass acid into the paper. Attachments such as pins, blu-tac, staples and self-adhesive tape can cause staining and damage.

- Some insects, such as silverfish, can graze on the surface of paper. The exit holes of woodworm may be found in books.
- Rodents like to use paper for nests; dogs often chew book bindings, as they like the animal glue; cats may use books for scratching posts; and snails consume paper.
- Paint, charcoal and pastels can become powdery or flake off.
- The structure of photographs is complex and so they are susceptible to a number of problems. The image can easily be lost if the photograph is not stored or displayed correctly.
- Books may contain leather and other materials that deteriorate. Leather is prone to damage from insects that eat proteinaceous materials while paper is not. Leather also weakens and becomes red and powdery, either as a result of its original manufacturing process and/or from pollution in the atmosphere.
- The boards of a book are usually larger than the text block and this can cause strain on the spine and joints, so that eventually the text block becomes loose. This is a particular problem for albums and thick books, so try to lie them flat. Poorly ventilated, warped and overcrowded shelving for books will cause physical damage.

Handling

If the paper is fragile, do not pick it up by one edge or by the corners; instead slide a sheet of card or blotting paper underneath the work and hold that piece instead. To turn it over, provided the surface is sound, place another sheet on top and make a sandwich. If you cannot avoid handling the piece itself, hold it by two opposite sides so that the paper does not flop or hang down. Do not touch the surface if it is delicate or when it is decorated with paint, chalk, charcoal or crayon.

Ideally, photographic prints should be kept in individual enclosures or envelopes made from clear polyester film (*see* p.104) so that there is no need to handle them directly.

The best way to remove a book from a shelf is to reach to the fore-edge and gently pull the book towards you, provided your hands will fit between the top of the book and the shelf. If there is no space for your hand, push the books that are on either side of the book you want further back into the shelf. This will allow you to get a better grip on the sides of the book. Do not pull by grabbing the top or the sides of the spine, as this will eventually break the book. Books which have folding maps, documents, plates or tables in them need to be handled carefully, as these inserts tear very easily. Open these items as little as possible, and fold them up following the original order and folds.

Display

The safest way to display photographs, works of art on paper and similar items is to put them in a frame made using archival-quality or acid-free materials and sealed to protect them against insects and dust.

When hanging frames, use picture wire rather than string, as it is stronger. If you are hanging pictures on an exterior wall, make sure that the picture is not completely flat against the wall by placing a spacer, such as a 1-cm (½in) piece of cork, between the frame and the wall. This will allow the air to circulate round the back of the frame, which is important as the wall may be slightly damp. The spacer can be attached directly to the frame with an easily reversible adhesive.

Storage

Paper-based objects should be protected from dust and kept in the dark, away from heat and damp. Boxes made from acid-free materials are best for storing unframed paper; they come in various sizes and designs and can be made to measure for particular objects. You can also buy or make simple box folders out of acid-free card yourself if you have only a few items to keep. Store the folders horizontally to prevent the paper from slipping to the bottom. Artists' portfolios are not ideal, as they are not made from archival-quality materials, do not always keep out the dust and insects, and can buckle. They are not a bad option, however, for large items. A simple wrapper made out of archive or acid-free card and tied with cotton tape will protect fragile books, or those that have part of the cover missing.

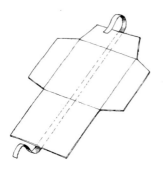

To make a folder: draw the outline of the folder, making sure it is larger than your object. Cut out the folder and score the card with a blunt knife along the lines where you want it to bend. Use white cotton tape to tie the folder closed.

Always remove paperclips, rubber bands, pins and (if possible) self-adhesive tape, mouldy or damaged mounts before putting items into a box. Place a layer of acid-free paper or tissue between unmounted objects and, if you have some items that are mounted and some not, keep them separate.

Photographic prints are stored in clear polyester film enclosures so that they can be easily examined. These enclosures can also be used for documents, ephemera etc. Avoid polyvinyl chloride (PVC) enclosures as PVC gives off vapours that are harmful to the film. For photographic film, the best material is silversafe paper or a similar product designed for the preservation of photographs.

Photograph albums can let dust and dirt in through the pages so, if possible, wrap them in clean cotton or linen sheeting or put them in acid-free boxes.

Good ventilation in a bookcase is essential, so leave a gap of 2.5cm (1in) between the back of the shelf and the wall. If you have bookshelves on an outside wall, this gap is extremely important. Some permanent shelves are built directly against the external wall, so to give ventilation drill holes of 2.5cm (1in) diameter at intervals along the back of the shelf. Of course you will have to consider carefully whether you want to drill into antique or very valuable shelves – a question of the practical versus the aesthetic.

Housekeeping & Maintenance

Brush the dust off framed pieces and wipe over the glass with a dry microfibre cloth when you can see just a little dust. How often you have to do this will depend on where you live, the season and other environmental factors. Pastel, chalk or charcoal drawings are very fragile and the pigment can be lifted up by static electricity, so do not polish the glass that frames this type of object. Check stored items from time to time for dust and make sure there is no mould, insect or other damage. Dust books and bookshelves regularly, taking the books off the shelves so you can check for woodworm, silverfish, mould, etc.

Do not open dirty books until the dust and grime have first been removed. Gently brush the dust off the top edge and then the other edges with a soft brush. Use a hogshair brush to remove the dust and dirt from near the headband. Clean the sides of the cover and the spine with a soft brush. If the books are in excellent condition, you may prefer to use a soft, clean duster or a dry microfibre cloth.

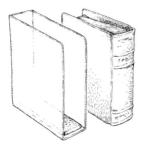

Check to see whether the books are beginning to sag and if they need a book-shoe. The book shoe, as shown left, is like a slipcase, without a top and including a textblock support.

Leather dressing

Many people used to rub leather dressing into their book bindings to protect the leather. In fact, the dressing can cause considerable harm, increasing the rate of deterioration of the leather and gathering dust and dirt, which act as abrasives to the binding. Best to avoid.

Cleaning

Cleaning paper-based objects is a tricky process and you can cause quite a lot of damage by the use of inappropriate materials or methods. The paper can stain or tear; the ink, pigment or paint can be smudged or lost; and the overall appearance can actually be made worse. Similarly, attempting to remove wax or grease marks can simply make the stain more unsightly. Therefore, for any very precious items, as well as all photographs, watercolours and drawings, work with a professional paper conservator.

CLEANING PRINTS

Some surface cleaning can be carried out on your less important prints and drawings (but not on hand-coloured prints), provided that the paper is in good condition, is not soft or fibrous, and where the ink will not be rubbed off.

You will need:

- a clean, flat surface;
- 2 sheets of clean, white blotting paper;
- a weight such as a clean tile, fairly heavy book, paperweight;
- a soft, clean sable brush;
- a dry chemical sponge cut into convenient-sized pieces.

1 Place a sheet of blotting paper on the table and then place the picture on top.
2 Remove surface dust from the picture with the sable brush.
3 Secure one end of the paper with the weight to stop it slipping, placing some blotting paper between the weight and the picture.
4 Use the margin to test how successful the cleaning will be: gently move a piece of sponge across the paper in straight lines and in one direction only. If this does not lift up the fibres or cause other damage, continue across the rest of the picture. Keep the sponge moving in straight lines, slightly overlapping each 'row'.

5 Turn the sponge over as soon as it gets dirty and use another piece of sponge when both sides are dirty.

N.B. Even when only one area of the print seems dirty, you should clean the whole surface, otherwise it will look patchy. You may need to go over the surface more than once, but do not continue if the paper fibres begin to raise or loosen.

Repair

Paper objects can be severely damaged by a poor repair and, as for all materials, it is essential to understand the nature of what you are working with and the risks posed. Do not attempt to repair old, rare or precious works on paper, drawings with loose pigments such as charcoal or pastels, or very weak or brittle paper yourself. Instead, take them to a paper conservator.

Repairing less precious prints and documents yourself is not without difficulty, because even if you use the correct materials there is still the risk of increased staining, smudging and cockling, and you can cause the ink to run and the paints to discolour. If you do decide to take the plunge, practice on some rough paper first and repair the tear only if the tear is seriously weakening the object and it cannot be supported by the frame.

MENDING A SMALL TEAR

Never use self-adhesive tape for repairing paper; the adhesive penetrates the paper, deteriorates and produces an indelible stain. Instead use the starch paste and Japanese paper method described below. Starch paste is very durable and should not cause any damage. Make sure the paste is not too wet, however, as water will be absorbed by the print and stain it. (The method can also be used on books but restrict this to books of little value or importance, as the process can easily go wrong.)

Starch paste recipe

100g (4oz) pure starch (arrowroot, wheat or rice flour)
800ml (30fl oz) distilled or deionised water

Mix the starch to a smooth cream with a little of the water in a glass or ceramic bowl. Boil the rest of the water and pour the boiling water into the cream, stirring continuously.

Heat the cream over a pan of simmering water and stir until it thickens. Continue to heat it for a further 10 minutes, then remove from the heat and pour into a lidded glass storage jar. Cover the top of the paste with a waxed paper disc such as used for jam-making, to prevent a skin from forming. The paste will keep for a few days in the refrigerator. If it starts to smell or go runny or mouldy, do not use it.

You will need:

◊ Japanese paper or acid-free tissue;
◊ starch paste (*see* box p.109);
◊ a clean, smooth surface such as a glass sheet or laminated surface;
◊ various clean, dry, soft artist's paintbrushes;
◊ a little water;
◊ tweezers;
◊ clean, white blotting paper;
◊ a piece of silicone paper;
◊ a small sheet of glass;
◊ a weight.

1 Remove dust from both sides of the paper with the soft artist's brush and lay the paper face down on the surface.

2 Adjust the tear so that it fits together closely, making sure any overlap of the tear is on the correct side. Use the artist's paintbrush to manipulate the paper.

3 Tear a strip of Japanese or acid-free tissue paper slightly longer than the tear and about 2mm wider on each side. Paint the outline of the required shape with water and a fine brush.

4 Pull the excess paper away from the piece that you want. Do not cut the paper.

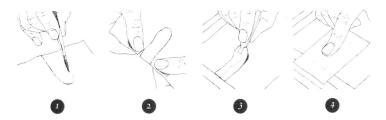

5   Place the patch of tissue paper on a piece of clean glass.
6   Paint on the paste so a thin film covers the entire surface.
7   Lift the paper patch with tweezers and lay it gently over the tear, ensuring that the edges of the tear remain close together. Gently pat the patch into place with your finger.
8   Place a piece of blotting paper under the tear and cover it with a piece of silicone paper.
9   Lightly rub the tear through the silicone paper to smooth the patch, then remove the silicone paper.
10 Cover the tear with clean blotting paper.
11 Place a sheet of glass over the blotting paper and put a light weight on top of the glass. Leave for at least 10 minutes.

With long tears, you should carry out the repair in stages, starting at the inner end and working towards the outside. Do not overlap the patches, but let them butt up to each other. There should be no gaps between the patches.

MOUNTING & FRAMING

Works on paper are protected by being mounted and framed. The frame is made of a moulding, often of wood or metal, a backing board, and the glass. The mount is the card on which the print or photograph is placed; generally the object is attached to the mount. There is usually also a card 'frame' or 'overmount' hinged to the back mount or 'backboard'. The mounted image is placed inside the frame, the backing board is then secured in position and finally the gap between the backing board and the frame moulding is covered with gummed paper tape.

All the materials used in the framing should be of archival quality. The gummed paper tape helps seal the frame to prevent insects and dust getting into the frame. Avoid self-adhesive tape because the adhesive can fail very quickly. If you are asking someone else to mount and frame your items, ask for 'conservation' framing. This way you will know that archival quality materials are being used, and that the object will be sealed against insects and dust.

The backboard mount is larger than the object and the overmount is the same size as the backboard. The overmount has an opening cut into it, which exposes the image but protects it from touching the glass. Occasionally a third sheet of card is used to cover the overmount. This protects the work when it is not on display. You can turn this sheet to the back when you want to display the picture.

A lot of damage can be caused to paper by poor mounting. Non-archival board can expose the object to acid vapours and deteriorate the paper. Old

mounting board, self-adhesive tape, dry-mounting tissues and dry-mounting sprays, as well as the adhesives used to attach the mounting hinges to the picture, can all stain or otherwise damage the paper. Note that very often less valuable works are more likely to be produced on unstable paper, which particularly needs the protection of the archival-quality board.

The backboard is usually of four-ply thickness, as is the overmount. (The overmount must be thick enough to hold the print or drawing well away from the glass.) The overall size of the mount should be a little larger than the artwork and the margins of the overmount need to be in proportion with the image – this is often best judged by eye. As a guide, a picture of about 50 x 40cm (20 x 16in) can take a 6.5–7.5cm (2½–3in) margin. The proportion of the margins may differ for some types of artwork: photographs are often mounted with narrow margins, while modern lithographs may have wider ones.

The backboard and overmount should be hinged together on the top or left-hand side with a strip of paper or fine fabric such as lawn or linen tape. Do not stick the two pieces of card directly together, as you need to be able to open the mount to remove or adjust the object.

The works on paper are attached to the mount with hinges or guards made from Japanese or acid-free tissue paper and starch paste. Alternatively, gummed linen tape can be used (but do not use self-adhesive tape). Some conservation suppliers sell Japanese tissue specially prepared so that it can be torn into strips to make hinges. An 'L' hinge is the easiest system to use

on small prints, as it is made up of a folded strip of paper placed at the top of both corners of the print. Make up the starch paste and apply it to the hinge, then place the hinge in position and press it down as described on pp.110–11. 'Drop hinges' are often used on larger or heavier objects. With a drop hinge, the paper is not folded and there is a second strip of paper going across the 'L' hinges to help secure them in place. As the hinges are not folded back under the object, the overmount will have to cover the edge of the print so that the hinges do not show.

FRAMING

A frame's backing board can be made from layers of four-ply acid-free board or other suitable archival-quality boards. Conservation suppliers will stock a range of boards and can advise you. Avoid hardboard, marine ply or cardboard for the backing board, as the acidity may stain and discolour the paper. Dust and insects can be kept out of the frame by sealing the back round the edge of the frame and the backing board with gummed paper tape, or gummed conservation framing tape. You can also use the gummed tape to seal around the inside edge of the glass and the rebate.

Floors

W ood, stone (including limestone, marble and slate), tile, plaster and cement are all used to make floors, while carpet, fibre matting (rush, sisal, coir, palm, straw and similar materials), cork tiles, Linoleum, and other sheet flooring (vinyl, rubber, etc.) are common floor coverings. Less common coverings include leather, glass, metal and fabric. Floors can also be painted.

Laminate flooring is popular, as it is durable, easy to lay and needs little maintenance. It is made up of a core of processed particle board, such as high-density fibre board (hdf), of different strengths and thicknesses. This is then sandwiched between two layers of resin-saturated paper. This structure means that the floor does not move as much as real wood flooring would when the humidity fluctuates, and can be easily wiped clean.

Cork flooring has been used in Europe for over a hundred years. Taken from the bark of the cork tree, it often has a tough urethane finish and is very resistant to dents and scratches. Cork is also a good insulator.

Vinyl flooring developed from Linoleum, which was made from linseed oil mixed with various resins and fillers on a cloth backing. The design of vinyl flooring is a printed image attached to a vinyl backing, and with a wear layer of vinyl or urethane.

Problems

The most common problems with floors are:

- Physical damage from use: scratches, marks, wear;
- Staining from spills of food and drink, and ingrained dirt and stains from use;
- Insect damage on carpets, rush matting and wood;
- Rot and decay where there is no damp-proof course under the floor or where there is another source of damp;
- Damage from exposure to sunlight for light-sensitive organic materials such as such as rush, leather and carpet.

Feet & Floors

You'll need to pay careful attention to your footwear if you want your floors to be in the best possible condition. So beware stiletto heels! The metal tip of the heel exerts very high pressure and will damage most types of flooring.

floors

Handling

For mats, rugs and carpets *see* Textiles.

Display & Storage

Direct sunlight will weaken the fibres as well as change the colour of your carpets and rugs. Light-sensitive flooring can be protected by using blinds and curtains when the room is not in use (see Introduction, p.9), and try to get into the habit of moving rugs from room to room or within a room so that the sunlight does not always fall on the same area. Very special rugs, carpets and other flooring can be protected from light and wear by using a drugget, which is a heavy cotton fabric laid over the carpet. In reality, few of us will want to go to these lengths, so must accept that the colours of our rugs and carpets will fade over time.

Damp is the other main enemy of floor coverings. It is especially common in old houses with stone and tile floors, particularly those laid directly on the earth without an effective damp-proof course. A heavy-duty damp-proof paper should be laid between the floor and the covering if the floor is likely to be damp.

Housekeeping & Maintenance

Keeping floors free of grit, grime and dust is essential for general maintenance and is most easily carried out using a vacuum cleaner. Upright vacuum cleaners usually have a rotating brush to pick up the dirt; this may be effective but can be too aggressive for most domestic floors and

118

is not recommended. Cylinder vacuum cleaners are preferable, as they just suck the dirt up without brushing. They usually have a head that can be adjusted so that you have a smooth setting for carpets, rugs and matting, but with the option of a small brush for hard flooring. Rugs and matting may occasionally need to have the dirt loosened by tamping before being vacuumed so that all the dirt and dust is sucked away (*see* p.71).

HARD FLOORS

First you need to remove all the loose dust and grit. Do not go straight for the mop, as it is much harder to remove all the dirt in this way. Also, if the dirt gets wet and then dries, it will make your job even more difficult.

A brush or broom is useful for picking up the loose dirt, particularly for small areas, but is not as efficient as a vacuum cleaner. A very useful addition to the floor cleaning toolkit is a microfibre or 'static' mop; these are now readily available and are used dry to pick up dust, grit and dirt. The microfibre mop can also be used damp for light dirt.

Revive waxed floors by wiping over with a cloth dampened with vinegar. To save working on your hands and knees, wring out the cloth and wrap it around a floor brush.

Cleaning

When washing modern floors, your best bet is to follow the instructions supplied by the manufacturers or installers. Bear in mind, however, that many of the cleaners or 'clean and shine' products recommended for modern floors are not suitable for historic or old floors, or for laminate, as they contain damaging chemicals and some contain silica that gives an inappropriate shine. The silica can also build up around the skirting board and in areas that are not heavily used, producing an unpleasant surface that is very difficult to remove.

WASHING FLOORS

Move as much furniture as you can out of the way and roll back the edge of rugs.

- Wash old stone, wood and Linoleum floors with a sponge dampened with a washing solution of water containing a small amount of conservation-grade detergent. In the past, timber floorboards would be scrubbed with damp sand, but this is not really practical today – there are easier options!
- Laminate floors can be cleaned with a solution of vinegar and water- or citrus-based cleaners, but do not use household detergents or abrasive cleaners.
- If you find that your floor cleans sufficiently with water alone, that's fine. There's no point adding unnecessary chemicals.
- Avoid getting the floor very wet – use the mop damp rather than wet.
- Wash around the feet of any furniture that you cannot move by hand. This will prevent the feet from getting damp, which will discolour them.

STAINS

Stains are very difficult to remove without making the appearance of the flooring worse, so if you have a badly stained floor seek advice from a conservator working with the appropriate material (stone, wood, etc.) or a building conservator.

Protection

Place a mat by the entrance doors to pick up the gravel and dust from people's shoes. Research shows that it takes about 3 metres (10 feet) of matting to be certain that most of the dirt has been removed from shoes. This is rather more than most of us have space for, but do use a mat that is larger than the traditional doormat if this is practical and aesthetically acceptable. Vacuum the mat regularly and occasionally beat it to remove the grit.

Hard floors such as tile and stone can become fragile and worn when they are old and may need protection. Rugs and matting are popular choices to protect hard floors, but do make sure they are cleaned underneath, otherwise the grit gathers between the floor and the covering and abrades the surface. Some floors can be marked by the protective covering itself – for example, sisal can leave marks on wood floors – so it is advisable to use carpet paper underneath the rug or matting.

Protect the floor from being scratched by furniture, particularly chairs, by placing felt pads under the feet. Carpets and flooring are easily marked by furniture with small feet or castors because the feet support a lot of weight that is concentrated in a small area. Furniture cups or a circle of MDF placed under the feet can help prevent this.

If you are having any building work done, or moving major items of furniture around, protect your floors by putting down sheets of clean, smooth plywood, hardboard or polypropylene twinwall board. You may need to hold the board in place with a strong tape (test first to make sure the tape will not damage the floor when it is pulled off). Where possible, place household equipment on a 'dolly' – a low platform with wheels – so items can be rolled rather than dragged.

SEALING

Modern stone and terracotta tile floors are usually sealed to protect them from staining. Use a sealant recommended by the supplier of the floor or a reputable flooring company. The sealant usually needs to be reapplied at intervals, as recommended by the manufacturer.

Avoid using sealant on old floors. Old buildings may not have been damp-proofed, and even if they have, the damp-proof is probably not very efficient, which means water vapour can pass through the floor. Sealing the floor will prevent this and could cause the floor to break up.

WAXING

Wood floors can be protected by a wax. Beeswax gives a pleasant shine, but in areas that have a lot of use a non-slip 'Traffic' wax may be more effective. Use a small amount of wax to avoid a build-up and re-wax regularly, particularly over heavily used areas. Manufacturers of laminate flooring advise you not to wax it.

Repairs

WOOD FLOORS

Wood floors may develop cracks over time. Before filling in a crack, observe the floor carefully through the seasons to see if the crack opens and closes according to changes in climate and humidity. If you can see a difference between, say, the winter and spring, be wary of filling in the cracks – the wood will continue to move and your filler will be deformed or, if the filler is hard, the wood will crack elsewhere.

If you feel confident that it is safe to fill the crack, use a suitably coloured wax paste and push it into the crack with a plastic or wood spatula. You may need to add more wax at a later date, as the paste will shrink.

The string and wax method

This is a method traditionally used to deal with large cracks in wood. The string is used to fill in the lower portions of large cracks and the wax is added as a layer on top. Sometimes floorboards are laid with an unattractively large gap between them. The best way of improving this is to take up the boards and relay them. However, if you do not want to do this then the string and wax method is useful.

STONE FLOORS

Stone floors can crumble and flake, particularly where they are worn. If your stone floor is suffering in this way, it should be remedied as soon as possible. You may be able to do this using a lime mortar mix, but seek advice from a stone conservator. Traditionally lime mortar was used for the grouting and pointing of floors and should be used on old floors. Unless you are familiar with using lime mortar, you should seek advice from a stone conservator.

REPAIRING FLOOR TILES AND MOSAICS

Tiles and mosaics often work themselves loose. Once this starts, the damage will simply get worse until the loose tiles are re-attached. To do this:

1 Remove the loose tile or tessera (piece of mosaic);
2 Clean out all loose material from the tile's space and the back of the tile;
3 Choose the right type of grout for your floor and mix the grout according to the instructions on the packet. Wear gloves to protect your hands;
4 Apply the grout in two or three blobs and place the tile in position. Push it down so that it is level in the floor. It should neither stick up above the other tiles nor be more sunken. If you need more grout, remove the tile and add a little more; conversely if the tile is sitting too high, remove some of the grout.

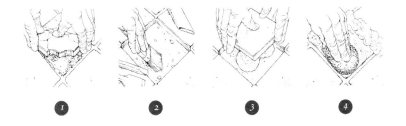

5 If the floor was originally laid with cement or a coloured grout you may need to adjust the colour of the grout when you point the tiles (ie fill in the space between the tiles). Do this by adding in small quantities of powder pigments or paint (which can be found in good hardware shops or art suppliers) to the grout. Raw umber is useful for making the grout look old and used. Mix the powder colour into the wet grout and check the colour once a little of the grout is dry, as the mixture will dry to a paler colour. Make sure that any grout on the surface of the tile is removed before it has dried.

index

accessories 61, 65
accumulated polish 54
adhesives 36
aerosol polishes 91
animal-derived fibres 59

biodeterioration 11
biscuit porcelain 19, 27
books 99-102, 105-6, 109
brass 33, 35, 37-8, 40
Britannia metal 45-6, 48
bronze 33, 35, 37, 39

candlesticks 34, 53
carpet beetles 60
carpets 10, 59, 61-5, 67,
    70-1, 74, 117-19, 121
cast iron 40
cedarwood 7, 72
central heating 9
ceramics 16-31, 81, 85
chairs 8, 84, 95, 121
chemical damage 10
chests 84
cleaning 14-15
    ceramics 24-7
    floors 119-21
    furniture 94-5
    metals 35, 37-8, 42,
        47-8, 50-4, 56-7
    paper 106-8

rug 70-1
    textiles 73-9
clothes 60-1, 65
codex books 99
conservation 5-6, 112, 114
conservators 15
    ceramics 24, 26-7
    floors 121, 124
    furniture 94-5
    metals 35-6, 39, 42,
        47, 55
    paper 106, 108
    textiles 69, 74, 77, 79
copper 33, 35-40, 45, 49
cork flooring 116
corrosion 10, 12-13, 33-4,
    36, 39-43, 45, 48-50,
    53, 55-6
curtains 8, 59-60, 85, 118

damp 13, 41, 49, 59, 61,
    63, 82, 103, 117-18,
    122
decoration 13, 54
deterioration 11, 13
display 10, 12-13
    ceramics 21-2
    floors 118
    furniture 85-7
    metals 34, 46
    paper 103

textiles 61-5
doormats 121
druggets 118
dry cleaning 74-5
dusters 15, 89-90, 105
dusting 24, 87-9, 93-4

earthenware 17-18, 24,
    26-7, 30
electrochemical cleaning
    54
electrum 48

fastenings 61, 65
fibres 59
filters 8
floors 10, 61, 115-25
flowers 86-7
footwear 117
framing 10, 112-14
French polish 86, 91, 93
furniture 8, 12-13, 15, 21,
    71, 80-97, 120-2

gases 10, 33
glazes 19, 24-5
gloves 12, 21, 34, 38, 46,
    50

handling 12-13, 59
    ceramics 21

floors 118
furniture 84
metals 34, 46
paper 102
textiles 62
hanging, carpets 64-5
hanging textiles 63
hard floors 119
health and safety 6, 72, 93
housekeeping 7, 24
floors 118-19
furniture 87-93
metals 34-5, 37, 41,
47, 50, 56
paper 105-6
textiles 69-73
humidity 9, 82, 85, 100,
123

insects 7, 13, 59-60, 65,
71-3, 78, 83, 88, 92-3,
101, 103, 105, 114,
117
iron 40-1, 44, 55-6
ironing 78

japanning 8, 81, 83

lacquers 8, 81, 91, 93, 97
laminate flooring 116,
120, 123

lavender 7, 72-3
lead 45-6, 48
leather 81, 91-2, 101, 106,
117
light 8, 59-60, 65, 82-3,
85, 100, 117-18

maintenance
ceramics 24
floors 118-19
furniture 87-93
metals 34-5, 37, 41,
47, 50, 56
paper 105-6
textiles 69-73
marquetry 81, 89, 96
metals 10-13, 32-57, 61,
63, 65, 81
mosaics 124-5
moth 60
mould 11, 13, 59, 61, 82,
100, 104-5
mounting 100, 112-14

paper 8-9, 11, 98-114
Parian ware 19, 27
parquetry 81
patina 37, 45, 48, 90
pests 7, 59
pewter 33, 45-8

photographs 99-100,
102-4, 106
physical damage 7
pinchbeck 37
plant fibres 59
plants 86-7
plastic furniture 87-8
polishing 39, 51-2, 90-1
pollution 10, 13, 61, 65
porcelain 17-19, 24-5
prints 99
problems 7-11
ceramics 19-20
floors 117
furniture 82-3
metals 39, 41, 45, 49
paper 100
textiles 59
protection 40, 43-4, 55,
121-3

red wine stains 79
repair 15
ceramics 27-30
floors 123-5
furniture 95-7
metals 35-7, 55
paper 108-14
textiles 79
restoration 5
rolling textiles 67-9

rugs 61, 63, 67, 70-1,
 118-19
rust 33-4, 41-3, 55

sealing 122
shellac 86, 91
silk 71, 77, 88
silver 35-6, 48-54
silverfish 60, 101, 105
soluble salts 22
spills 78-9
stab stitching 66
stainless steel 41, 43
stains 78-9, 108, 117,
 121-2
starch 78
starch paste recipe 109
steel 33, 40-3
sterling silver 48
stiletto heels 117
stone 10-11, 61, 81, 116,
118, 120, 122, 124
stoneware 17-18, 24-5, 30
storage 10, 12-13
 ceramics 23
 floors 118
 furniture 85-7
 metals 34, 46
 paper 103-5
 textiles 61, 65

string and wax method
 123
synthetic fibres 59

tables 84-5
tarnish 34-6, 39-40, 49-55
tears 51, 102, 106, 108-11
temperature 9-10
terracotta 10, 26, 61, 122
textiles 7-9, 58-79, 81-2
three-dimensional textiles
 59
tiles 22, 30-1, 116, 118,
 122, 124-5
tin/tinplate 55-7
two-dimensional textiles
 59, 62-5

underlay 62

veneer 9, 13, 15, 81-2,
 87-9, 96
vinyl flooring 116

washing floors 120
watering plants 86-7
wax 9-10, 35, 90-1, 122-3
Wedgwood, Josiah 17-18
wet cleaning 74-7
wood 11, 61

floors 63, 116-17, 120,
 122-3
 furniture 81-3, 90, 94
woodworm 92, 101, 105
wrought iron 41